Nathaniel Hawthorne

Transformation

Nathaniel Hawthorne

Transformation

ISBN/EAN: 9783741162985

Manufactured in Europe, USA, Canada, Australia, Japa

Cover: Foto ©Thomas Meinert / pixelio.de

Manufactured and distributed by brebook publishing software
(www.brebook.com)

Nathaniel Hawthorne

Transformation

TRANSFORMATION:

OR, THE

ROMANCE OF MONTE BENI.

BY

NATHANIEL HAWTHORNE,

AUTHOR OF "THE SCARLET LETTER," ETC. ETC.

COPYRIGHT EDITION.

IN TWO VOLUMES.

VOL. I.

LEIPZIG

BERNHARD TAUCHNITZ

1860.

PREFACE.

It is now seven or eight years (so many, at all events, that I cannot precisely remember the epoch) since the author of this romance last appeared before the Public. It had grown to be a custom with him to introduce each of his humble publications with a familiar kind of preface, addressed nominally to the Public at large, but really to a character with whom he felt entitled to use far greater freedom. He meant it for that one congenial friend—more comprehensive of his purposes, more appreciative of his success, more indulgent of his shortcomings, and, in all respects, closer and kinder than a brother—that all sympathizing critic, in short, whom an author never actually meets, but to whom he implicitly makes his appeal whenever he is conscious of having done his best.

The antique fashion of Prefaces recognized this genial personage as the "Kind Reader," the "Gentle Reader," the "Beloved," the "Indulgent," or, at coldest, the "Honoured Reader," to whom the prim old author was wont to make his preliminary explanations and apologies, with the certainty that they would be favourably received. I never personally encountered, nor corresponded through the post with this representative essence of all delightful and desirable qualities which a reader can possess. But, fortunately for myself, I never therefore concluded him to be merely a mythic character. I had always a sturdy faith in his actual existence, and wrote for him year after year, during which the great eye of the Public (as well it might) almost utterly overlooked my small productions.

Unquestionably, this gentle, kind, benevolent, indulgent, and most beloved and honoured Reader did once exist for me, and (in spite of the infinite chances against a letter's reaching its destination without a definite address) duly received the scrolls which I flung upon whatever wind was blowing, in the faith that they would find him out. But, is he extant now? In these many years, since he last heard from me, may he not have deemed his earthly task accomplished, and have withdrawn to the paradise of gentle readers, wherever it may be, to the enjoyments of which his kindly charity on my behalf must surely have entitled him? I have a sad foreboding that this may be the truth. The "Gentle Reader," in the case of any individual author, is apt to be extremely short-lived; he seldom outlasts a literary fashion, and, except in very rare instances, closes his weary eyes before the writer has half done with him. If I find him at all, it will probably be under some mossy gravestone, inscribed with a half-obliterated name which I shall never recognize.

Therefore, I have little heart or confidence (especially, writing as I do, in a foreign land, and after a long, long absence from my own) to presume upon the existence of that friend of friends, that unseen brother of the soul, whose apprehensive sympathy has so often encouraged me to be egotistical in my prefaces, careless though unkindly eyes should skim over what was never meant for them. I stand upon ceremony, now; and, after stating a few particulars about the work which is here offered to the Public, must make my most reverential bow, and retire behind the curtain.

This Romance was sketched out during a residence of considerable length in Italy, and has been re-written and prepared for the press in England. The author proposed to himself merely to write a fanciful story, evolving a thoughtful moral, and did not purpose attempting a portraiture of Italian manners and character. He has lived too long abroad not to be aware that a foreigner seldom acquires that knowledge of a country, at once flexible and profound, which may justify him in endeavouring to idealize its traits.

Italy, as the site of his Romance, was chiefly valuable to him as affording a sort of poetic or fairy precinct, where actualities would not be so terribly insisted upon as they are, and must needs be, in America. No author, without a trial, can conceive of the difficulty of writing a romance about a country where there is no shadow, no antiquity, no mystery, no picturesque and gloomy wrong, nor anything but a common-place prosperity, in broad and simple daylight, as is happily the case with my dear native land. It will be very long, I trust, before romance-writers may find congenial and easily handled themes either in the annals of our stalwart republic, or in any characteristic and probable events of our individual lives. Romance and poetry, ivy, lichens, and wall-flowers, need ruin to make them grow.

In re-writing these volumes, the author was somewhat surprised to see the extent to which he had introduced descriptions of various Italian objects, antique, pictorial, and statuesque. Yet these things fill the mind everywhere in Italy, and especially in Rome, and cannot easily be kept from flowing out upon the page when one writes freely, and with self-enjoyment. And, again, while reproducing the book, on the broad and dreary sands of Redcar, with the gray German Ocean tumbling in upon me, and the northern blast always howling in my ears, the complete change of scene made these Italian reminiscences shine out so vividly that I could not find it in my heart to cancel them.

An act of justice remains to be performed towards two men of genius with whose productions the author has allowed himself to use a quite unwarrantable freedom. Having imagined a sculptor in this Romance, it was necessary to provide him with such works in marble as should be in keeping with the artistic ability which he was supposed to possess. With this view, the author laid felonious hands upon a certain bust of Milton, and a statue of a pearl-diver, which he found in the studio of Mr. PAUL AKERS, and secretly conveyed them to the premises of his imaginary friend, in the Via Frezza. Not content even with these spoils, he committed a further robbery upon a magnificent statue of Cleopatra, the production of Mr. WILLIAM W. STORY, an artist whom his country and the world will not long fail to appreciate. He had thoughts of appropriating, likewise, a certain door of bronze by Mr. RANDOLPH ROGERS, representing the history of Columbus in a series of admirable bas-reliefs, but was deterred by an unwillingness to meddle with public property. Were he capable of stealing from a lady, he would certainly have made free with Miss HOSMER's noble statue of Zenobia.

He now wishes to restore the above-mentioned beautiful pieces of sculpture to their proper owners, with many thanks, and the avowal of his sincere admiration. What he has said of them in the Romance does not partake of the fiction in which they are imbedded, but expresses his genuine opinion, which he has little doubt will be found in accordance with that of the Public. It is, perhaps, unnecessary to say, that, while stealing their designs, the Author has not taken a similar liberty with the personal characters of either of these gifted sculptors; his own man of marble being entirely imaginary.

Leamington, December 15, 1859.

CONTENTS

OF VOLUME I.

		Page
CHAPTER I.	Miriam, Hilda, Kenyon, Donatello	1
— II.	The Faun	9
— III.	Subterranean Reminiscences	19
— IV.	The Spectre of the Catacomb	28
— V.	Miriam's Studio	40
— VI.	The Virgin's Shrine	57
— VII.	Beatrice	70
— VIII.	The Suburban Villa	80
— IX.	The Faun and Nymph	88
— X.	The Sylvan Dance	98
— XI.	Fragmentary Sentences	107
— XII.	A Stroll on the Pincian	116
— XIII.	A Sculptor's Studio	134
— XIV.	Cleopatra	146
— XV.	An Æsthetic Company	156
— XVI.	A Moonlight Ramble	169
— XVII.	Miriam's Trouble	183
— XVIII.	On the Edge of a Precipice	193
— XIX.	The Faun's Transformation	207
— XX.	The Burial Chaunt	215

		Page
CHAPTER XXI.	The Dead Capuchin	226
— XXII.	The Medici Gardens	236
— XXIII.	Miriam and Hilda	245
— XXIV.	The Tower among the Apennines	258
— XXV.	Sunshine	267
— XXVI.	The Pedigree of Monte Beni	279

THE ROMANCE OF MONTE BENI.

VOL. I.

CHAPTER I.

Miriam, Hilda, Kenyon, Donatello.

Four individuals, in whose fortunes we should be glad to interest the reader, happened to be standing in one of the saloons of the sculpture-gallery in the Capitol at Rome. It was that room (the first, after ascending the staircase) in the centre of which reclines the noble and most pathetic figure of the Dying Gladiator, just sinking into his death-swoon. Around the walls stand the Antinous, the Amazon, the Lycian Apollo, the Juno; all famous productions of antique sculpture, and still shining in the undiminished majesty and beauty of their ideal life, although the marble that embodies them is yellow with time, and perhaps corroded by the damp earth in which they lay buried for centuries. Here, likewise, is seen a symbol (as apt at this moment as it was two thousand years ago) of the Human Soul, with its choice of Innocence or Evil close at hand, in the pretty figure of a child, clasping a dove to her bosom, but assaulted by a snake.

From one of the windows of this saloon, we may see a flight of broad stone steps, descending alongside the antique and massive foundation of the Capitol, towards the battered triumphal arch of Septimius Severus, right below. Farther on, the eye skirts along the edge of the desolate Forum (where Roman washerwomen hang out their linen to the sun), passing over a shapeless confusion of modern edifices, piled rudely up with ancient brick and stone, and over the domes of Christian churches, built on the old pavements of heathen temples, and supported by the very pillars that once upheld them. At a distance beyond—yet but a little way, considering how much history is heaped into the intervening space—rises the great sweep of the Coliseum, with the blue sky brightening through its upper tier of arches. Far off, the view is shut in by the Alban mountains, looking just the same, amid all this decay and change, as when Romulus gazed thitherward over his half-finished wall.

We glance hastily at these things—at this bright sky, and those blue, distant mountains, and at the ruins, Etruscan, Roman, Christian, venerable with a threefold antiquity, and at the company of world-famous statues in the saloon—in the hope of putting the reader into that state of feeling which is experienced oftenest at Rome. It is a vague sense of ponderous remembrances; a perception of such weight and density in a bygone life, of which this spot was the centre, that the present moment is pressed down or crowded out, and our individual affairs and interests are but half as real here as elsewhere. Viewed through this medium, our narrative—into which are woven some airy and unsubstantial threads, intermixed with others, twisted out of the commonest stuff of human existence—may seem not widely different from the texture of all our lives.

Side by side with the massiveness of the Roman Past, all matters that we handle or dream of now-a-days look evanescent and visionary alike.

It might be that the four persons whom we are seeking to introduce, were conscious of this dreamy character of the present, as compared with the square blocks of granite wherewith the Romans built their lives. Perhaps it even contributed to the fanciful merriment which was just now their mood. When we find ourselves fading into shadows and unrealities, it seems hardly worth while to be sad, but rather to laugh as gaily as we may, and ask little reason wherefore.

Of these four friends of ours, three were artists, or connected with art; and, at this moment, they had been simultaneously struck by a resemblance between one of the antique statues, a well-known masterpiece of Grecian sculpture, and a young Italian, the fourth member of their party.

"You must needs confess, Kenyon," said a dark-eyed young woman, whom her friends called Miriam, "that you never chiselled out of marble, nor wrought in clay, a more vivid likeness than this, cunning a bust-maker as you think yourself. The portraiture is perfect in character, sentiment, and feature. If it were a picture, the resemblance might be half illusive and imaginary; but here, in this Pentelic marble, it is a substantial fact, and may be tested by absolute touch and measurement. Our friend Donatello is the very Faun of Praxiteles. Is it not true, Hilda?"

"Not quite—almost—yes, I really think so," replied Hilda, a slender, brown-haired, New England girl, whose perceptions of form and expression were wonderfully clear and delicate. "If there is any difference between the two faces the reason may be, I suppose, that the Faun dwelt in woods and fields, and consorted with his like; whereas, Donatello has known cities a little, and such people as ourselves. But the resemblance is very close, and very strange."

"Not so strange," whispered Miriam, mischievously; "for no Faun in Arcadia was ever a greater simpleton than Donatello. He has hardly a man's share of wit, small as that may be. It is a pity there are no longer any of this congenial race of rustic creatures for our friend to consort with!"

"Hush, naughty one!" returned Hilda. "You are very ungrateful, for you well know he has wit enough to worship you, at all events."

"Then the greater fool he!" said Miriam, so bitterly that Hilda's quiet eyes were somewhat startled.

"Donatello, my dear friend," said Kenyon, in Italian, "pray gratify us all by taking the exact attitude of this statue."

The young man laughed, and threw himself into the position in which the statue has been standing for

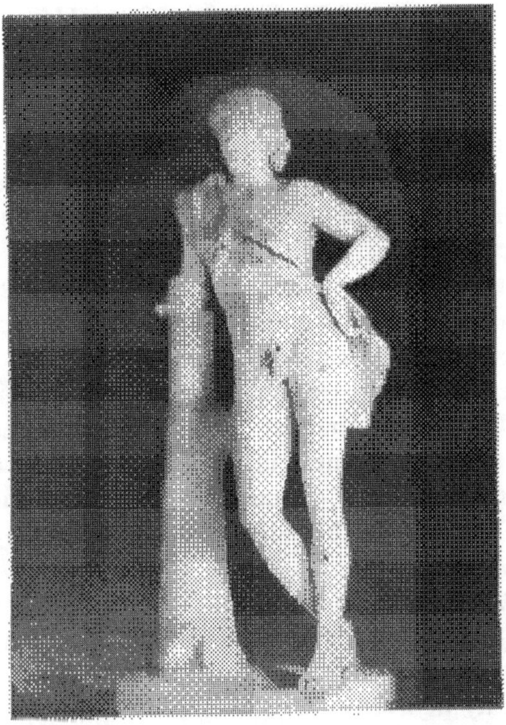

two or three thousand years. In truth, allowing for the difference of costume, and if a lion's skin could have been substituted for his modern talma, and a rustic pipe for his stick, Donatello might have figured perfectly as the marble Faun, miraculously softened into flesh and blood.

"Yes; the resemblance is wonderful," observed Kenyon, after examining the marble and the man with the accuracy of a sculptor's eye. "There is one point, however, or, rather, two points, in respect to which our friend Donatello's abundant curls will not permit us to say whether the likeness is carried into minute detail."

And the sculptor directed the attention of the party to the ears of the beautiful statue which they were contemplating.

But we must do more than merely refer to this exquisite work of art; it must be described, however inadequate may be the effort to express its magic peculiarity in words.

The Faun is the marble image of a young man, leaning his right arm on the trunk or stump of a tree; one hand hangs carelessly by his side, in the other he holds the fragment of a pipe, or some such sylvan instrument of music. His only garment—a lion's skin, with the claws upon his shoulder—falls half way down his back, leaving the limbs and entire front of the figure nude. The form, thus displayed, is marvellously graceful, but has a fuller and more rounded outline, more flesh, and less of heroic muscle than the old sculptors were wont to assign to their types of masculine beauty. The character of the face corresponds with the figure; it is most agreeable in outline and feature, but rounded and somewhat voluptuously developed, especially about the throat and chin; the nose is almost straight, but very slightly curves inward, thereby acquiring an indescribable charm of geniality and humour. The mouth, with its full yet delicate lips, seems so nearly to smile outright, that it calls forth a responsive smile. The whole statue—unlike anything else that ever was wrought in that severe material of marble—conveys the idea of an amiable and sensual creature, easy, mirthful, apt for jollity, yet not incapable of being touched by pathos. It is impossible to gaze long at this stone image without conceiving a kindly sentiment towards it, as if its substance were warm to the touch, and imbued with actual life. It comes very close to some of our pleasantest sympathies.

Perhaps it is the very lack of moral severity, of any high and heroic ingredient in the character of the Faun, that makes it so delightful an object to the human eye and to the frailty of the human heart. The being here represented is endowed with no principle of virtue, and would be incapable of comprehending such; but he would be true and honest by dint of his simplicity. We should expect from him no sacrifice or effort for an abstract cause; there is not an atom of martyr's stuff in all that softened marble; but he has a capacity for strong and warm attachment, and might act devotedly through its impulse, and even die for it at need. It is possible, too, that the Faun might be educated through the medium of his emotions, so that the coarser animal portion of his nature might eventually be thrown into the background, though never utterly expelled.

The animal nature, indeed, is a most essential part of the Faun's composition; for the characteristics of the brute creation meet and combine with those of humanity in this strange yet true and natural conception of antique poetry and art. Praxiteles has subtly diffused throughout his work that mute mystery which so hopelessly perplexes us whenever we attempt to gain an intellectual or sympathetic knowledge of the lower orders of creation. The riddle is indicated, however, only by two definite signs; these are the two ears of the Faun, which are leaf-shaped, terminating in little peaks, like those of some species of animals. Though not so seen in the marble, they are probably to be considered as clothed in fine, downy fur. In the coarser representations of this class of mythological creatures, there is another token of brute kindred—a certain caudal appendage; which, if the Faun of Praxiteles must be supposed to possess it at all, is hidden by the lion's skin that forms his garment. The pointed and furry ears, therefore, are the sole indications of his wild, forest nature.

Only a sculptor of the finest imagination, the most delicate taste, the sweetest feeling, and the rarest artistic skill—in a word, a sculptor and a poet too—could have first dreamed of a Faun in this guise, and then have succeeded in imprisoning the sportive and frisky thing in marble. Neither man nor animal, and yet no monster; but a being in whom both races meet on friendly ground! The idea grows coarse as we handle it, and hardens in our grasp. But, if the spectator broods long over the statue, he will be conscious of its spell; all the pleasantness of sylvan life, all the genial and happy characteristics of creatures that dwell in woods and fields, will seem to be mingled and kneaded into one substance, along with the kindred qualities in the human soul. Trees, grass, flowers, woodland streamlets, cattle, deer, and unsophisticated man! The essence of all these was compressed long ago, and still exists within that discoloured marble surface of the Faun of Praxiteles.

And, after all, the idea may have been no dream, but rather a poet's reminiscence of a period when man's affinity with nature was more strict, and his fellowship with every living thing more intimate and dear.

CHAPTER II.

The Faun.

"DONATELLO," playfully cried Miriam, "do not leave us in this perplexity! Shake aside those brown curls, my friend, and let us see whether this marvellous resemblance extends to the very tips of the ears. If so, we shall like you all the better!"

"No, no, dearest signorina," answered Donatello, laughing, but with a certain earnestness. "I entreat you to take the tips of my ears for granted." As he spoke, the young Italian made a skip and jump, light enough for a veritable faun; so as to place himself quite beyond the reach of the fair hand that was outstretched, as if to settle the matter by actual examination. "I shall be like a wolf of the Apennines," he continued, taking his stand on the other side of the Dying Gladiator, "if you touch my ears ever so softly. None of my race could endure it. It has always been a tender point with my forefathers and me."

He spoke in Italian, with the Tuscan rusticity of accent, and an unshaped sort of utterance, betokening that he must heretofore have been chiefly conversant with rural people.

"Well, well," said Miriam, "your tender point—your two tender points, if you have them—shall be safe, so far as I am concerned. But how strange this likeness is, after all! and how delightful, if it really includes the pointed ears! Oh, it is impossible, of course," she continued, in English, "with a real and common-place young man like Donatello; but you see how this peculiarity defines the position of the Faun; and, while putting him where he cannot exactly assert his brotherhood, still disposes us kindly towards the kindred creature. He is not supernatural, but just on the verge of nature, and yet within it. What is the nameless charm of this idea, Hilda? You can feel it more delicately than I."

"It perplexes me," said Hilda, thoughtfully, and shrinking a little; "neither do I quite like to think about it."

"But, surely," said Kenyon, "you agree with Miriam and me, that there is something very touching and impressive in this statue of the Faun. In some long past age, he must really have existed. Nature needed, and still needs, this beautiful creature; standing betwixt man and animal, sympathizing with each, comprehending the speech of either race, and interpreting the whole existence of one to the other. What a pity that he has for ever vanished from the hard and dusty paths of life—unless," added the sculptor, in a sportive whisper, "Donatello be actually he!"

"You cannot conceive how this fantasy takes hold of me," responded Miriam, between jest and earnest. "Imagine, now, a real being, similar to this mythic Faun; how happy, how genial, how satisfactory would be his life, enjoying the warm, sensuous, earthy side of nature; revelling in the merriment of woods and streams; living as our four-footed kindred do — as mankind did in its innocent childhood: before sin, sorrow, or morality itself had ever been thought of! Ah! Kenyon, if Hilda, and you, and I—if I, at least —had pointed ears! For I suppose the Faun had no conscience, no remorse, no burthen on the heart, no troublesome recollections of any sort; no dark future either."

"What a tragic tone was that last, Miriam!" said the sculptor, and, looking into her face, he was startled to behold it pale and tear-stained. "How suddenly this mood has come over you!"

"Let it go as it came," said Miriam, "like a thunder-shower in this Roman sky. All is sunshine again, you see!"

Donatello's refractoriness as regarded his ears had evidently cost him something, and he now came close to Miriam's side, gazing at her with an appealing air, as if to solicit forgiveness. His mute, helpless gesture of entreaty had something pathetic in it, and yet might well enough excite a laugh, so like it was to what you may see in the aspect of a hound when he thinks himself in fault or disgrace. It was difficult to make out the character of this young man. So full of animal life as he was, so joyous in his deportment, so handsome, so physically well developed, he made no impression of incompleteness, of maimed or stinted nature. And yet, in social intercourse, these familiar friends of his habitually and instinctively allowed for him, as for a child or some other lawless thing, exacting no strict obedience to conventional rules, and hardly noticing his eccentricities enough to pardon them. There was an indefinable characteristic about Donatello that set him outside of rules.

He caught Miriam's hand, kissed it, and gazed into her eyes without saying a word. She smiled, and bestowed on him a little, careless caress, singularly like what one would give to a pet dog when he puts himself in the way to receive it. Not that it was so decided a caress either, but only the merest touch, somewhere between a pat and a tap of the finger; it might be a mark of fondness, or perhaps a playful pretence of punishment. At all events, it appeared to afford Donatello exquisite pleasure; insomuch that he danced quite round the wooden railing that fences in the Dying Gladiator.

"It is the very step of the Dancing Faun," said Miriam apart to Hilda. "What a child, or what a simpleton, he is! I continually find myself treating Donatello as if he were the merest unfledged chicken; and yet he can claim no such privileges in the right of his tender age; for he is at least—how old should you think him, Hilda?"

"Twenty years, perhaps," replied Hilda, glancing at Donatello; "but, indeed, I cannot tell; hardly so old, on second thoughts, or possibly older. He has nothing to do with time, but has a look of eternal youth in his face."

"All underwitted people have that look," said Miriam, scornfully.

"Donatello has certainly the gift of eternal youth, as Hilda suggests," observed Kenyon, laughing; "for, judging by the date of this statue, which, I am more and more convinced Praxiteles carved on purpose for him, he must be at least twenty-five centuries old, and he still looks as young as ever."

"What age have you, Donatello?" asked Miriam.

"Signorina, I do not know," he answered; "no great age, however; for I have only lived since I met you."

"Now, what old man of society could have turned a silly compliment more smartly than that!" exclaimed Miriam. "Nature and art are just at one sometimes. But what a happy ignorance is this of our friend Donatello! Not to know his own age! It is equivalent to being immortal on earth. If I could only forget mine!"

"It is too soon to wish that," observed the sculptor; "you are scarcely older than Donatello looks."

"I shall be content, then," rejoined Miriam, "if I could only forget one day of all my life." Then she seemed to repent of this allusion, and hastily added, "A woman's days are so tedious that it is a boon to leave even one of them out of the account."

The foregoing conversation had been carried on in a mood in which all imaginative people, whether artists or poets, love to indulge. In this frame of mind, they sometimes find their profoundest truths side by side with the idlest jest, and utter one or the other, apparently without distinguishing which is the most valuable or assigning any considerable value to either. The resemblance between the marble Faun and their living companion had made a deep, half-serious, half-mirthful impression on these three friends, and had taken them into a certain airy region, lifting up, as it is so pleasant to feel them lifted, their heavy earthly feet from the actual soil of life. The world had been set afloat, as it were, for a moment, and relieved them for just so long of all customary responsibility for what they thought and said.

It might be under this influence — or, perhaps, because sculptors always abuse one another's works — that Kenyon threw in a criticism upon the Dying Gladiator.

"I used to admire this statue exceedingly," he remarked, "but, latterly, I find myself getting weary and annoyed that the man should be such a length of time leaning on his arm in the very act of death. If he is so terribly hurt, why does he not sink down and die without further ado? Flitting moments, imminent emergencies, imperceptible intervals between two breaths, ought not to be encrusted with the eternal repose of marble; in any sculptural subject, there should be a moral standstill, since there must of necessity be a physical one. Otherwise, it is like flinging a block of marble up into the air, and by some trick or enchantment, causing it to stick there. You feel that it ought to come down, and are dissatisfied that it does not obey the natural law."

"I see," said Miriam, mischievously, "you think that sculpture should be a sort of fossilizing process. But, in truth, your frozen art has nothing like the scope and freedom of Hilda's and mine. In painting there is no similar objection to the representation of brief snatches of time; perhaps, because a story can be so much more fully told in picture, and buttressed about with circumstances that give it an epoch. For instance, a painter never would have sent down yonder Faun out of his far antiquity, lonely and desolate, with no companion to keep his simple heart warm."

"Ah, the Faun!" cried Hilda, with a little gesture of impatience; "I have been looking at him too long; and now, instead of a beautiful statue, immortally young, I see only a corroded and discoloured stone. This change is very apt to occur in statues."

"And a similar one in pictures, surely," retorted the sculptor. "It is the spectator's mood that transfigures the Transfiguration itself. I defy any painter to move and elevate me without my own consent and assistance."

"Then you are deficient of a sense," said Miriam.

The party now strayed onward from hall to hall of that rich gallery, pausing here and there, to look at the multitude of noble and lovely shapes, which have been dug up out of the deep grave in which old Rome lies buried. And, still, the realization of the antique Faun, in the person of Donatello, gave a more vivid character to all these marble ghosts. Why should not each statue grow warm with life! Antinous might lift his brow, and tell us why he is for ever sad. The Lycian Apollo might strike his lyre; and, at the first vibration, that other Faun in red marble, who keeps up a motionless dance, should frisk gaily forth, leading yonder Satyrs, with shaggy goat-shanks, to clatter their little hoofs upon the floor, and all join hands with Donatello! Bacchus, too, a rosy flush diffusing itself over his time-stained surface, could come down from his pedestal, and offer a cluster of purple grapes to Donatello's lips; because the god recognizes him as the woodland elf who so often shared his revels. And here, in this sarcophagus, the exquisitely carved figures might assume life, and chase one another round its verge with that wild merriment which is so strangely represented on those old burial coffers; though still with some subtle allusion to death, carefully veiled, but for ever peeping forth amid emblems of mirth and riot.

As the four friends descended the stairs, however, their play of fancy subsided into a much more sombre mood; a result apt to follow upon such exhilaration as that which had so recently taken possession of them.

"Do you know," said Miriam, confidentially to Hilda, "I doubt the reality of this likeness of Donatello to the Faun, which we have been talking so much about? To say the truth, it never struck me so forcibly as it did Kenyon and yourself, though I gave in to whatever you were pleased to fancy, for the sake of a moment's mirth and wonder."

"I was certainly in earnest, and you seemed equally so," replied Hilda, glancing back at Donatello, as if to reassure herself of the resemblance. "But faces change so much, from hour to hour, that the same set of features has often no keeping with itself; to an eye, at least, which looks at expression more than outline. How sad and sombre he has grown, all of a sudden!"

"Angry too, methinks! nay, it is anger much more than sadness," said Miriam. "I have seen Donatello in this mood once or twice before. If you consider him well, you will observe an odd mixture of the bull-dog, or some other equally fierce brute, in our friend's composition; a trait of savageness hardly to be expected in such a gentle creature as he usually is. Donatello is a very strange young man. I wish he would not haunt my footsteps so continually."

"You have bewitched the poor lad," said the sculptor, laughing. "You have a faculty of bewitching people, and it is providing you with a singular train of followers. I see another of them behind yonder pillar; and it is his presence that has aroused Donatello's wrath."

They had now emerged from the gateway of the palace; and partly concealed by one of the pillars of the portico, stood a figure such as may often be encountered in the streets and piazzas of Rome, and nowhere else. He looked as if he might just have stept out of a picture, and, in truth, was likely enough to find his way into a dozen pictures; being no other than one of those living models, dark, bushy-bearded, wild of aspect and attire, whom artists convert into saints or assassins, according as their pictorial purposes demand.

"Miriam," whispered Hilda, a little startled, "it is your model!"

CHAPTER III.

Subterranean Reminiscences.

Miriam's model has so important a connection with our story, that it is essential to describe the singular mode of his first appearance, and how he subsequently became a self-appointed follower of the young female artist. In the first place, however, we must devote a page or two to certain peculiarities in the position of Miriam herself.

There was an ambiguity about this young lady, which, though it did not necessarily imply anything wrong, would have operated unfavourably as regarded her reception in society, anywhere but in Rome. The truth was, that nobody knew anything about Miriam, either for good or evil. She had made her appearance without introduction, had taken a studio, put her card upon the door, and showed very considerable talent as a painter in oils. Her fellow-professors of the brush, it is true, showered abundant criticisms upon her pictures, allowing them to be well enough for the idle half-efforts of an amateur, but lacking both the trained skill and the practice that distinguish the works of a true artist.

Nevertheless, be their faults what they might, Miriam's pictures met with good acceptance among the patrons of modern art. Whatever technical merit they lacked, its absence was more than supplied by a warmth and passionateness, which she had the faculty of putting into her productions, and which all the world could feel. Her nature had a great deal of colour, and, in accordance with it, so likewise had her pictures.

Miriam had great apparent freedom of intercourse; her manners were so far from evincing shyness, that it seemed easy to become acquainted with her, and not difficult to develop a casual acquaintance into intimacy. Such, at least, was the impression which she made, upon brief contact, but not such the ultimate conclusion of those who really sought to know her. So airy, free, and affable was Miriam's deportment towards all who came within her sphere, that possibly they might never be conscious of the fact; but so it was, that they did not get on, and were seldom any farther advanced into her good graces to-day than yesterday. By some subtle quality, she kept people at a distance, without so much as letting them know that they were excluded from her inner circle. She resembled one of those images of light, which conjurors evoke and cause to shine before us, in apparent tangibility, only an arm's length beyond our grasp: we make a step in advance, expecting to seize the illusion, but find it still precisely so far out of our reach. Finally, society began to recognize the impossibility of getting nearer to Miriam, and gruffly acquiesced.

There were two persons, however, whom she appeared to acknowledge as friends in the closer and truer sense of the word; and both of these more favoured individuals did credit to Miriam's selection. One was a young American sculptor, of high promise and rapidly increasing celebrity; the other, a girl of the same country, a painter like Miriam herself, but in a widely different sphere of art. Her heart flowed out towards these two; she requited herself by their society and friendship (and especially by Hilda's) for all the loneliness with which, as regarded the rest of the world, she chose to be surrounded. Her two friends were conscious of the strong, yearning grasp which Miriam laid upon them, and gave her their affection in full measure; Hilda, indeed, responding with the fervency of a girl's first friendship, and Kenyon with a manly regard, in which there was nothing akin to what is distinctively called love.

A sort of intimacy subsequently grew up between these three friends and a fourth individual; it was a young Italian, who, casually visiting Rome, had been attracted by the beauty which Miriam possessed in a remarkable degree. He had sought her, followed her, and insisted, with simple perseverance, upon being admitted at least to her acquaintance; a boon which had been granted, when a more artful character, seeking it by a more subtle mode of pursuit, would probably have failed to obtain it. This young man, though anything but intellectually brilliant, had many agreeable characteristics which won him the kindly and half-contemptuous regard of Miriam and her two friends. It was he whom they called Donatello, and whose wonderful resemblance to the Faun of Praxiteles forms the key-note of our narrative.

Such was the position in which we find Miriam some few months after her establishment at Rome. It must be added, however, that the world did not permit her to hide her antecedents without making her the subject of a good deal of conjecture; as was natural enough, considering the abundance of her personal charms, and the degree of notice that she attracted as an artist. There were many stories about Miriam's origin and previous life, some of which had a very probable air, while others were evidently wild and romantic fables. We cite a few, leaving the reader to designate them either under the probable or the romantic head.

It was said, for example, that Miriam was the daughter and heiress of a great Jewish banker (an idea perhaps suggested by a certain rich Oriental character in her face), and had fled from her paternal home to escape a union with a cousin, the heir of another of that golden brotherhood; the object being, to retain their vast accumulation of wealth within the family. Another story hinted, that she was a German princess, whom, for reasons of state, it was proposed to give in marriage either to a decrepit sovereign, or a prince still in his cradle. According to a third statement, she was the offspring of a Southern American planter, who had given her an elaborate education and endowed her with his wealth; but the one burning drop of African blood in her veins so affected her with a sense of ignominy, that she relinquished all, and fled her country. By still another account she was the lady of an English nobleman; and, out of mere love and honour of art, had thrown aside the splendour of her rank, and come to seek a subsistence by her pencil in a Roman studio.

In all the above cases, the fable seemed to be instigated by the large and bounteous impression which Miriam invariably made, as if necessity and she could have nothing to do with one another. Whatever deprivations she underwent must needs be voluntary. But there were other surmises, taking such a commonplace view as that Miriam was the daughter of a merchant or financier, who had been ruined in a great commercial crisis; and, possessing a taste for art, she had attempted to support herself by the pencil, in preference to the alternative of going out as governess.

Be these things how they might, Miriam, fair as she looked, was plucked up out of a mystery, and had its roots still clinging to her. She was a beautiful and attractive woman, but based, as it were, upon a cloud, and all surrounded with misty substance; so that the result was to render her sprite-like in her most ordinary manifestations. This was the case even in respect to Kenyon and Hilda, her especial friends. But such was the effect of Miriam's natural language, her generosity, kindliness, and native truth of character, that these two received her as a dear friend into their hearts, taking her good qualities as evident and genuine, and never imagining that what was hidden must be therefore evil.

We now proceed with our narrative.

The same party of friends, whom we have seen at the sculpture gallery of the Capitol, chanced to have gone together, some months before, to the catacomb of St. Calixtus. They went joyously down into that vast tomb, and wandered by torchlight through a sort of dream, in which reminiscences of church-aisles and grimy cellars—and chiefly the latter—seemed to be broken into fragments, and hopelessly intermingled. The intricate passages along which they followed their guide had been hewn, in some forgotten age, out of a dark-red, crumbly stone. On either side were horizontal niches, where, if they held their torches closely, the shape of a human body was discernible in white ashes, into which the entire mortality of a man or woman had resolved itself. Among all this extinct dust, there might perchance be a thigh-bone, which crumbled at a touch; or possibly a skull, grinning at its own wretched plight, as is the ugly and empty habit of the thing.

Sometimes their gloomy pathway tended upward, so that, through a crevice, a little daylight glimmered down upon them, or even a streak of sunshine peeped into a burial niche; then again, they went downward by gradual descent, or by abrupt, rudely hewn steps, into deeper and deeper recesses of the earth. Here and there the narrow and tortuous passages widened somewhat, developing themselves into small chapels; which once, no doubt, had been adorned with marble-work and lighted with ever-burning lamps and tapers. All such illumination and ornament, however, had long since been extinguished and stript away; except, indeed, that the low roofs of a few of these ancient sites of worship were covered with dingy stucco, and frescoed with scriptural scenes and subjects, in the dreariest stage of ruin.

In one such chapel, the guide showed them a low arch, beneath which the body of St. Cecilia had been buried after her martyrdom, and where it lay till a sculptor saw it, and rendered it for ever beautiful in marble.

In a similar spot they found two sarcophagi, one containing a skeleton, and the other a shrivelled body, which still wore the garments of its former lifetime.

"How dismal all this is!" said Hilda, shuddering. "I do not know why we came here, nor why we should stay a moment longer."

"I hate it all!" cried Donatello, with peculiar energy. "Dear friends, let us hasten back into the blessed daylight!"

From the first, Donatello had shown little fancy for the expedition; for, like most Italians, and in especial accordance with the law of his own simple and physically happy nature, this young man had an infinite repugnance to graves and skulls, and to all that ghastliness which the Gothic mind loves to associate with the idea of death. He shuddered, and looked fearfully round, drawing nearer to Miriam, whose attractive influence alone had enticed him into that gloomy region.

"What a child you are, poor Donatello!" she observed, with the freedom which she always used towards him. "You are afraid of ghosts!"

"Yes, signorina; terribly afraid!" said the truthful Donatello.

"I also believe in ghosts," answered Miriam, "and could tremble at them, in a suitable place. But these sepulchres are so old, and these skulls and white ashes so very dry, that methinks they have ceased to be haunted. The most awful idea connected with the catacombs is their interminable extent, and the possibility of going astray into this labyrinth of darkness, which broods around the little glimmer of our tapers."

"Has any one ever been lost here?" asked Kenyon of the guide.

"Surely, signor; one, no longer ago than my father's time," said the guide; and he added, with the air of a man who believed what he was telling, "but the first that went astray here was a pagan of old Rome, who hid himself in order to spy out and betray the blessed saints, who then dwelt and worshipped in these dismal places. You have heard the story, signor? A miracle was wrought upon the accursed one; and, ever since (for fifteen centuries at least), he has been groping in the darkness, seeking his way out of the catacomb."

"Has he ever been seen?" asked Hilda, who had great and tremulous faith in marvels of this kind.

"These eyes of mine never beheld him, signorina; the saints forbid!" answered the guide. "But it is well known that he watches near parties that come into the catacomb, especially if they be heretics, hoping to lead some straggler astray. What this lost wretch pines for, almost as much as for the blessed sunshine, is a companion to be miserable with him."

"Such an intense desire for sympathy indicates something amiable in the poor fellow, at all events," observed Kenyon.

They had now reached a larger chapel than those heretofore seen; it was of a circular shape, and though hewn out of the solid mass of red sandstone, had pillars, and a carved roof, and other tokens of a regular architectural design. Nevertheless, considered as a church, it was exceedingly minute, being scarcely twice a man's stature in height, and only two or three paces from wall to wall; and while their collected torches illuminated this one, small, consecrated spot, the great darkness spread all round it, like that immenser mystery which envelopes our little life, and into which friends vanish from us, one by one.

"Why, where is Miriam?" cried Hilda.

The party gazed hurriedly from face to face, and became aware that one of their party had vanished into the great darkness, even while they were shuddering at the remote possibility of such a misfortune.

CHAPTER IV.

The Spectre of the Catacomb.

"SURELY, she cannot be lost!" exclaimed Kenyon. "It is but a moment since she was speaking."

"No, no!" said Hilda, in great alarm. "She was behind us all; and it is a long while since we have heard her voice!"

"Torches! torches!" cried Donatello, desperately. "I will seek her, be the darkness ever so dismal!"

But the guide held him back, and assured them all, that there was no possibility of assisting their lost companion, unless by shouting at the very top of their voices. As the sound would go very far along these close and narrow passages, there was a fair probability that Miriam might hear the call, and be able to retrace her steps.

Accordingly, they all—Kenyon with his bass voice; Donatello with his tenor; the guide with that high and hard Italian cry, which makes the streets of Rome so resonant; and Hilda with her slender scream, piercing farther than the united uproar of the rest—began to shriek, halloo, and bellow, with the utmost force of their lungs. And, not to prolong the reader's suspense (for we do not particularly seek to interest him in this scene, telling it only on account of the trouble and strange entanglement which followed), they soon heard a responsive call, in a female voice.

"It was the signorina!" cried Donatello, joyfully.

"Yes; it was certainly dear Miriam's voice," said Hilda. "And here she comes! Thank Heaven! Thank Heaven!"

The figure of their friend was now discernible by her own torchlight, approaching out of one of the cavernous passages. Miriam came forward, but not with the eagerness and tremulous joy of a fearful girl, just rescued from a labyrinth of gloomy mystery. She made no immediate response to their inquiries and tumultuous congratulations; and, as they afterwards remembered, there was something absorbed, thoughtful, and self-concentrated in her deportment. She looked pale, as well she might, and held her torch with a nervous grasp, the tremor of which was seen in the irregular twinkling of the flame. This last was the chief perceptible sign of any recent agitation or alarm.

"Dearest, dearest Miriam," exclaimed Hilda, throwing her arms about her friend, "where have you been straying from us? Blessed be Providence, which has rescued you out of that miserable darkness!"

"Hush, dear Hilda!" whispered Miriam, with a strange little laugh. "Are you quite sure that it was Heaven's guidance which brought me back? If so, it was by an odd messenger, as you will confess. See; there he stands."

Startled at Miriam's words and manner, Hilda

gazed into the duskiness whither she pointed, and there beheld a figure standing just on the doubtful limit of obscurity, at the threshold of the small, illuminated chapel. Kenyon discerned him at the same instant, and drew nearer with his torch; although the guide attempted to dissuade him, averring that, once beyond the consecrated precincts of the chapel, the apparition would have power to tear him limb from limb. It struck the sculptor, however, when he afterwards recurred to these circumstances, that the guide manifested no such apprehension on his own account as he professed on behalf of others; for he kept pace with Kenyon as the latter approached the figure, though still endeavouring to restrain him.

In fine, they both drew near enough to get as good a view of the spectre as the smoky light of their torches, struggling with the massive gloom, could supply.

The stranger was of exceedingly picturesque, and even melodramatic aspect. He was clad in a voluminous cloak, that seemed to be made of a buffalo's hide, and a pair of those goatskin breeches, with the hair outward, which are still commonly worn by the peasants of the Roman Campagna. In this garb, they look like antique Satyrs; and, in truth, the Spectre of the Catacomb might have represented the last survivor of that vanished race, hiding himself in sepulchral gloom, and mourning over his lost life of woods and streams.

Furthermore, he had on a broad-brimmed, conical hat, beneath the shadow of which a wild visage was indistinctly seen, floating away, as it were, into a dusky wilderness of moustache and beard. His eyes winked, and turned uneasily from the torches, like a creature to whom midnight would be more congenial than noonday.

On the whole, the spectre might have made a considerable impression on the sculptor's nerves, only that he was in the habit of observing similar figures, almost every day, reclining on the Spanish steps, and waiting for some artist to invite them within the magic realm of picture. Nor, even thus familiarized with the stranger's peculiarities of appearance, could Kenyon help wondering to see such a personage, shaping himself so suddenly out of the void darkness of the catacomb.

"What are you?" said the sculptor, advancing his torch nearer. "And how long have you been wandering here?"

"A thousand and five hundred years!" muttered the guide, loud enough to be heard by all the party. "It is the old pagan phantom that I told you of, who sought to betray the blessed saints!"

"Yes; it is a phantom!" cried Donatello, with a shudder. "Ah, dearest signorina, what fearful thing has beset you, in those dark corridors!"

"Nonsense, Donatello," said the sculptor. "The man is no more a phantom than yourself. The only marvel is, how he comes to be hiding himself in the catacomb. Possibly, our guide might solve the riddle."

The spectre himself here settled the point of his

tangibility, at all events, and physical substance, by approaching a step nearer, and laying his hand on Kenyon's arm.

"Inquire not what I am, nor wherefore I abide in the darkness," said he, in a hoarse, harsh voice, as if a great deal of damp were clustering in his throat. "Henceforth, I am nothing but a shadow behind her footsteps. She came to me when I sought her not. She has called me forth, and must abide the consequences of my reappearance in the world."

"Holy Virgin! I wish the signorina joy of her prize," said the guide, half to himself. "And in any case, the catacomb is well rid of him."

We need follow the scene no farther. So much is essential to the subsequent narrative, that, during the short period while astray in those tortuous passages, Miriam had encountered an unknown man, and led him forth with her, or was guided back by him, first into the torchlight, thence into the sunshine.

It was the further singularity of this affair, that the connection, thus briefly and casually formed, did not terminate with the incident that gave it birth. As if her service to him, or his service to her, whichever it might be, had given him an indefeasible claim on Miriam's regard and protection, the Spectre of the Catacomb never long allowed her to lose sight of him, from that day forward. He haunted her footsteps with more than the customary persistency of Italian mendicants, when once they have recognized a benefactor. For days together, it is true, he occasionally vanished, but always reappeared, gliding after her through the narrow streets, or climbing the hundred steps of her staircase and sitting at her threshold.

Being often admitted to her studio, he left his features, or some shadow or reminiscence of them, in many of her sketches and pictures. The moral atmosphere of these productions was thereby so influenced, that rival painters pronounced it a case of hopeless mannerism, which would destroy all Miriam's prospects of true excellence in art.

The story of this adventure spread abroad, and made its way beyond the usual gossip of the Forestieri, even into Italian circles, where, enhanced by a still potent spirit of superstition, it grew far more wonderful than as above recounted. Thence, it came back among the Anglo-Saxons, and was communicated to the German artists, who so richly supplied it with romantic ornaments and excrescences, after their fashion, that it became a fantasy worthy of Tieck or Hoffman. For nobody has any conscience about adding to the improbabilities of a marvellous tale.

The most reasonable version of the incident, that could anywise be rendered acceptable to the auditors, was substantially the one suggested by the guide of the catacomb, in his allusion to the legend of Memmius. This man, or demon, or man-demon, was a spy during the persecutions of the early Christians, probably under the Emperor Diocletian, and penetrated into the catacomb of St. Calixtus, with the malignant purpose of tracing out the hiding-places of the refugees. But, while he stole craftily through those dark corridors, he chanced to come upon a little chapel, where tapers were burning before an altar and a crucifix, and a priest was in the performance of his sacred office. By divine indulgence, there was a single moment's grace allowed to Memmius, during which, had he been capable of Christian faith and love, he might have knelt before the cross, and received the holy light into his soul, and so have been blest for ever. But he resisted the sacred impulse. As soon, therefore, as that one moment had glided by, the light of the consecrated tapers, which represent all truth, bewildered the wretched man with everlasting error, and the blessed cross itself was stamped as a seal upon his heart, so that it should never open to receive conviction.

Thenceforth, this heathen Memmius has haunted the wide and dreary precincts of the catacomb, seeking, as some say, to beguile new victims into his own misery; but, according to other statements, endeavouring to prevail on any unwary visitor to take him by the hand, and guide him out into the daylight. Should his wiles and entreaties take effect, however, the man-demon would remain only a little while above ground. He would gratify his fiendish malignity by perpetrating signal mischief on his benefactor, and perhaps bringing some old pestilence or other forgotten and long-buried evil on society; or, possibly, teaching the modern world some decayed and dusty kind of crime, which the antique Romans knew; and then would hasten back to the catacomb, which, after so long haunting it, has grown his most congenial home.

Miriam herself, with her chosen friends, the sculptor and the gentle Hilda, often laughed at the monstrous fictions that had gone abroad in reference to her adventure. Her two confidants (for such they were, on all ordinary subjects) had not failed to ask an explanation of the mystery, since undeniably a mystery there was, and one sufficiently perplexing itself, without any help from the imaginative faculty. And, sometimes responding to their inquiries with a melancholy sort of playfulness, Miriam let her fancy run off into wilder fables than any which German ingenuity or Italian superstition had contrived.

For example, with a strange air of seriousness over all her face, only belied by a laughing gleam in her dark eyes, she would aver that the spectre (who had been an artist in his mortal lifetime) had promised to teach her a long lost, but invaluable secret of old Roman fresco-painting. The knowledge of this process would place Miriam at the head of modern art; the sole condition being agreed upon, that she should return with him into his sightless gloom, after enriching a certain extent of stuccoed wall with the most brilliant and lovely designs. And what true votary of art would not purchase unrivalled excellence, even at so vast a sacrifice!

Or, if her friends still solicited a soberer account,

Miriam replied, that, meeting the old infidel in one of the dismal passages of the catacomb, she had entered into controversy with him, hoping to achieve the glory and satisfaction of converting him to the Christian faith. For the sake of so excellent a result, she had even staked her own salvation against his, binding herself to accompany him back into his penal gloom, if, within a twelvemonth's space, she should not have convinced him of the errors through which he had so long groped and stumbled. But, alas! up to the present time, the controversy had gone direfully in favour of the man-demon; and Miriam (as she whispered in Hilda's ear) had awful forebodings, that, in a few more months, she must take an eternal farewell of the sun!

It was somewhat remarkable, that all her romantic fantasies arrived at this selfsame dreary termination; it appeared impossible for her even to imagine any other than a disastrous result from her connection with her ill-omened attendant.

This singularity might have meant nothing, however, had it not suggested a despondent state of mind, which was likewise indicated by many other tokens. Miriam's friends had no difficulty in perceiving that, in one way or another, her happiness was very seriously compromised. Her spirits were often depressed into deep melancholy. If ever she was gay, it was seldom with a healthy cheerfulness. She grew moody, moreover, and subject to fits of passionate ill-temper; which usually wreaked itself on the heads of those who loved her best. Not that Miriam's indifferent acquaintances were safe from similar outbreaks of her displeasure, especially if they ventured upon any allusion to the model. In such cases, they were left with little disposition to renew the subject, but inclined, on the other hand, to interpret the whole matter as much to her discredit as the least favourable colouring of the facts would allow.

It may occur to the reader, that there was really no demand for so much rumour and speculation in regard to an incident, which might well enough have been explained without going many steps beyond the limits of probability. The spectre might have been merely a Roman beggar, whose fraternity often harbour in stranger shelters than the catacombs; or one of those pilgrims, who still journey from remote countries to kneel and worship at the holy sites, among which these haunts of the early Christians are esteemed especially sacred. Or, as was perhaps a more plausible theory, he might be a thief of the city, a robber of the Campagna, a political offender, or an assassin, with blood upon his hand; whom the negligence or connivance of the police allowed to take refuge in those subterranean fastnesses, where such outlaws have been accustomed to hide themselves from a far antiquity downward. Or he might have been a lunatic, fleeing instinctively from man, and making it his dark pleasure to dwell among the tombs, like him whose awful cry echoes afar to us from Scripture times.

And, as for the stranger's attaching himself so devotedly to Miriam, her personal magnetism might be allowed a certain weight in the explanation. For what remains, his pertinacity need not seem so very singular to those who consider how slight a link serves to connect these vagabonds of idle Italy with any person that may have the illhap to bestow charity, or be otherwise serviceable to them, or betray the slightest interest in their fortunes.

Thus little would remain to be accounted for, except the deportment of Miriam herself; her reserve, her brooding melancholy, her petulance, and moody passion. If generously interpreted, even these morbid symptoms might have sufficient cause in the stimulating and exhausting influences of an imaginative art, exercised by a delicate young woman, in the nervous and unwholesome atmosphere of Rome. Such, at least, was the view of the case which Hilda and Kenyon endeavoured to impress on their own minds, and impart to those whom their opinions might influence.

One of Miriam's friends took the matter sadly to heart. This was the young Italian. Donatello, as we have seen, had been an eye-witness of the stranger's first appearance, and had ever since nourished a singular prejudice against the mysterious, dusky, death-scented apparition. It resembled not so much a human dislike or hatred, as one of those instinctive, unreasoning antipathies which the lower animals sometimes display, and which generally prove more trustworthy than the acutest insight into character. The shadow of the model, always flung into the light which Miriam diffused around her, caused no slight trouble to Donatello. Yet he was of a nature so remarkably genial and joyous, so simply happy, that he might well afford to have something subtracted from his comfort, and make tolerable shift to live upon what remained.

CHAPTER V.

Miriam's Studio.

THE courtyard and staircase of a palace built three hundred years ago, are a peculiar feature of modern Rome, and interest the stranger more than many things of which he has heard loftier descriptions. You pass through the grand breadth and height of a squalid entrance-way, and perhaps see a range of dusky pillars, forming a sort of cloister round the court, and in the intervals, from pillar to pillar, are strewn fragments of antique statues, headless and legless torsos, and busts that have invariably lost—what it might be well if living men could lay aside in that unfragrant atmosphere—the nose. Bas-reliefs, the spoil of some far older palace, are set in the surrounding walls, every stone of which has been ravished from the Coliseum, or any other imperial ruin which earlier barbarism had not already levelled with the earth. Between two of the pillars, moreover, stands an old sarcophagus without its lid, and with all its more prominently projecting sculptures broken off; perhaps it once held famous dust, and the bony framework of some historic man, although now only a receptacle for the rubbish of the courtyard, and a half-worn broom.

In the centre of the court, under the blue Italian

sky, and with the hundred windows of the vast palace gazing down upon it, from four sides, appears a fountain. It brims over from one stone basin to another, or gushes from a Naiad's urn, or spirts its many little jets from the mouths of nameless monsters, which were merely grotesque and artificial when Bernini, or whoever was their unnatural father, first produced them; but now the patches of moss, the tufts of grass, the trailing maiden-hair, and all sorts of verdant weeds that thrive in the cracks and crevices of moist marble, tell us that Nature takes the fountain back into her great heart, and cherishes it as kindly as if it were a woodland spring. And, hark, the pleasant murmur, the gurgle, the plash! You might hear just those tinkling sounds from any tiny waterfall in the forest, though here they gain a delicious pathos from the stately echoes that reverberate their natural language. So the fountain is not altogether glad, after all its three centuries of play!

In one of the angles of the courtyard, a pillared doorway gives access to the staircase, with its spacious breadth of low, marble steps, up which, in former times, have gone the princes and cardinals of the great Roman family who built this palace. Or they have come down, with still grander and loftier mien, on their way to the Vatican or the Quirinal, there to put off their scarlet hats in exchange for the triple crown. But, in fine, all these illustrious personages have gone down their hereditary staircase for the last time, leaving it to be the thoroughfare of ambassadors, English noblemen, American millionnaires, artists, tradesmen, washerwomen, and people of every degree; all of whom find such gilded and marble-panelled saloons as their pomp and luxury demand, or such homely garrets as their necessity can pay for, within this one multifarious abode. Only, in not a single nook of the palace (built for splendour, and the accommodation of a vast retinue, but with no vision of a happy fireside or any mode of domestic enjoyment) does the humblest or the haughtiest occupant find comfort.

Up such a staircase, on the morning after the scene at the sculpture gallery, sprang the light foot of Donatello. He ascended from story to story, passing lofty doorways, set within rich frames of sculptured marble, and climbing unweariedly upward, until the glories of the first piano and the elegance of the middle height were exchanged for a sort of Alpine region, cold and naked in its aspect. Steps of rough stone, rude wooden balustrades, a brick pavement in the passages, a dingy whitewash on the walls; these were here the palatial features. Finally, he paused before an oaken door, on which was pinned a card, bearing the name of Miriam Schaefer, artist in oils. Here Donatello knocked, and the door immediately fell somewhat ajar; its latch having been pulled up by means of a string on the inside. Passing through a little ante-room, he found himself in Miriam's presence.

"Come in, wild Faun," she said, "and tell me the latest news from Arcady!"

The artist was not just then at her easel, but was

busied with the feminine task of mending a pair of gloves.

There is something extremely pleasant, and even touching—at least, of very sweet, soft, and winning effect—in this peculiarity of needlework, distinguishing women from men. Our own sex is incapable of any such byplay aside from the main business of life; but women—be they of what earthly rank they may, however gifted with intellect or genius, or endowed with awful beauty—have always some little handiwork ready to fill the tiny gap of every vacant moment. A needle is familiar to the fingers of them all. A queen, no doubt, plies it on occasion; the woman-poet can use it as adroitly as her pen; the woman's eye, that has discovered a new star, turns from its glory to send the polished little instrument gleaming along the hem of her kerchief, or to darn a casual fray in her dress. And they have greatly the advantage of us in this respect. The slender thread of silk or cotton keeps them united with the small, familiar, gentle interests of life, the continually operating influences of which do so much for the health of the character, and carry off what would otherwise be a dangerous accumulation of morbid sensibility. A vast deal of human sympathy runs along this electric line, stretching from the throne to the wicker-chair of the humblest seamstress, and keeping high and low in a species of communion with their kindred beings. Methinks it is a token of healthy and gentle characteristics, when women of high thoughts and accomplishments love to sew; especially as they are never more at home with their own hearts than while so occupied.

And when the work falls in a woman's lap, of its own accord, and the needle involuntarily ceases to fly, it is a sign of trouble, quite as trustworthy as the throb of the heart itself. This was what happened to Miriam. Even while Donatello stood gazing at her, she seemed to have forgotten his presence, allowing him to drop out of her thoughts, and the torn glove to fall from her idle fingers. Simple as he was, the young man knew by his sympathies that something was amiss.

"Dear lady, you are sad," said he, drawing close to her.

"It is nothing, Donatello," she replied, resuming her work: "yes; a little sad, perhaps; but that is not strange for us people of the ordinary world, especially for women. You are of a cheerfuller race, my friend, and know nothing of this disease of sadness. But why do you come into this shadowy room of mine?"

"Why do you make it so shadowy?" asked he.

"We artists purposely exclude sunshine, and all but a partial light," said Miriam, "because we think it necessary to put ourselves at odds with nature before trying to imitate her. That strikes you very strangely, does it not? But we make very pretty pictures sometimes, with our artfully arranged lights and shadows. Amuse yourself with some of mine, Donatello, and by and by I shall be in the mood to begin the portrait we were talking about."

The room had the customary aspect of a painter's

studio; one of those delightful spots that hardly seem to belong to the actual world, but rather to be the outward type of a poet's haunted imagination, where there are glimpses, sketches, and half-developed hints of beings and objects grander and more beautiful than we can anywhere find in reality. The windows were closed with shutters, or deeply curtained, except one, which was partly open to a sunless portion of the sky, admitting only from high upward that partial light which, with its strongly marked contrast of shadow, is the first requisite towards seeing objects pictorially. Pencil-drawings were pinned against the wall or scattered on the tables. Unframed canvases turned their backs on the spectator, presenting only a blank to the eye, and churlishly concealing whatever riches of scenery or human beauty Miriam's skill had depicted on the other side.

In the obscurest part of the room Donatello was half startled at perceiving duskily a woman with long dark hair, who threw up her arms with a wild gesture of tragic despair, and appeared to beckon him into the darkness along with her.

"Do not be afraid, Donatello," said Miriam, smiling to see him peering doubtfully into the mysterious dusk. "She means you no mischief, nor could perpetrate any if she wished it ever so much. It is a lady of exceedingly pliable disposition; now a heroine of romance, and now a rustic maid; yet all for show; being created, indeed, on purpose to wear rich shawls and other garments in a becoming fashion. This is the true end of her being, although she pretends to assume the most varied duties and perform many parts in life, while really the poor puppet has nothing on earth to do. Upon my word, I am satirical unawares, and seem to be describing nine women out of ten in the person of my lay-figure. For most purposes she has the advantage of the sisterhood. Would I were like her!"

"How it changes her aspect," exclaimed Donatello, "to know that she is but a jointed figure. When my eyes first fell upon her, I thought her arms moved, as if beckoning me to help her in some direful peril."

"Are you often troubled with such sinister freaks of fancy?" asked Miriam. "I should not have supposed it."

"To tell you the truth, dearest signorina," answered the young Italian, "I am apt to be fearful in old, gloomy houses, and in the dark. I love no dark or dusky corners, except it be in a grotto, or among the thick green leaves of an arbour, or in some nook of the woods, such as I know many in the neighbourhood of my home. Even there, if a stray sunbeam steal in, the shadow is all the better for its cheerful glimmer."

"Yes; you are a Faun, you know," said the fair artist, laughing at the remembrance of the scene of the day before. "But the world is sadly changed now-a-days; grievously changed, poor Donatello, since those happy times when your race used to dwell in the Arcadian woods, playing hide-and-seek with the nymphs in grottoes and nooks of shrubbery. You have reappeared on earth some centuries too late."

"I do not understand you now," answered Donatello, looking perplexed; "only, signorina, I am glad to have my lifetime while you live; and where you are, be it in cities or fields, I would fain be there too."

"I wonder whether I ought to allow you to speak in this way," said Miriam, looking thoughtfully at him. "Many young women would think it behoved them to be offended. Hilda would never let you speak so, I dare say. But he is a mere boy," she added, aside, "a simple boy, putting his boyish heart to the proof on the first woman whom he chances to meet. If yonder lay-figure had had the luck to meet him first, she would have smitten him as deeply as I."

"Are you angry with me?" asked Donatello, dolorously.

"Not in the least," answered Miriam, frankly giving him her hand. "Pray look over some of these sketches till I have leisure to chat with you a little. I hardly think I am in spirits enough to begin your portrait to-day."

Donatello was as gentle and docile as a pet spaniel; as playful, too, in his general disposition, or saddening with his mistress's variable mood like that or any other kindly animal which has the faculty of bestowing its sympathies more completely than men or women can ever do. Accordingly, as Miriam bade him, he tried to turn his attention to a great pile and confusion of pen-and-ink sketches and pencil-drawings which lay tossed together on a table. As it chanced, however, they gave the poor youth little delight.

The first that he took up was a very impressive sketch, in which the artist had jotted down her rough ideas for a picture of Jael driving the nail through the temples of Sisera. It was dashed off with remarkable power, and showed a touch or two that were actually life-like and death-like, as if Miriam had been standing by when Jael gave the first stroke of her murderous hammer, or as if she herself were Jael, and felt irresistibly impelled to make her bloody confession in this guise.

Her first conception of the stern Jewess had evidently been that of perfect womanhood, a lovely form, and a high, heroic face of lofty beauty; but, dissatisfied either with her own work or the terrible story itself, Miriam had added a certain wayward quirk of her pencil, which at once converted the heroine into a vulgar murderess. It was evident that a Jael like this would be sure to search Sisera's pockets as soon as the breath was out of his body.

In another sketch she had attempted the story of Judith, which we see represented by the old masters so often, and in such various styles. Here, too, beginning with a passionate and fiery conception of the subject in all earnestness, she had given the last touches in utter scorn, as it were, of the feelings which at first took such powerful possession of her hand. The head of Holofernes (which by the by had a pair of twisted moustaches, like those of a certain potentate of the day) being fairly cut off, was screwing its eyes upward and twirling its features into a diabolical grin of triumphant malice, which it flung right in Judith's face. On her part, she had the startled aspect that might be conceived of a cook if a calf's head should sneer at her when about to be popped into the dinner-pot.

Over and over again, there was the idea of woman, acting the part of a revengeful mischief towards man. It was, indeed, very singular to see how the artist's imagination seemed to run on these stories of bloodshed, in which woman's hand was crimsoned by the stain; and how, too—in one form or another, grotesque or sternly sad—she failed not to bring out the moral, that woman must strike through her own heart to reach a human life, whatever were the motive that impelled her.

One of the sketches represented the daughter of Herodias receiving the head of John the Baptist in a charger. The general conception appeared to be taken from Bernardo Luini's picture, in the Uffizzi gallery at Florence; but Miriam had imparted to the saint's face a look of gentle and heavenly reproach, with sad and blessed eyes fixed upward at the maiden; by the force of which miraculous glance, her whole womanhood was at once awakened to love and endless remorse.

These sketches had a most disagreeable effect on Donatello's peculiar temperament. He gave a shudder; his face assumed a look of trouble, fear, and disgust; he snatched up one sketch after another, as if about to tear it in pieces. Finally, shoving away the pile of drawings, he shrank back from the table and clasped his hands over his eyes.

"What is the matter, Donatello?" asked Miriam, looking up from a letter which she was now writing. "Ah! I did not mean you to see those drawings. They are ugly phantoms that stole out of my mind; not things that I created, but things that haunt me. See! here are some trifles that perhaps will please you better."

She gave him a portfolio, the sketches in which indicated a happier mood of mind, and one, it is to be hoped, more truly characteristic of the artist. Supposing neither of these classes of subject to show anything of her own individuality, Miriam had evidently a great scope of fancy, and a singular faculty of putting what looked like heart into her productions. The latter sketches were domestic and common scenes, so finely and subtilely idealized that they seemed such as we may see at any moment, and everywhere; while still there was the indefinable something added, or taken away, which makes all the difference between sordid life and an earthly paradise. The feeling and sympathy in all of them were deep and true. There was the scene, that comes once in every life, of the lover winning the soft and pure avowal of bashful affection from the maiden, whose slender form half leans towards his arm, half shrinks from it, we know not which. There was wedded affection in its successive stages, represented in a series of delicately conceived designs, touched with a holy fire, that burned from youth to age in those two hearts, and gave one identical beauty to the faces, throughout all the changes of feature.

There was a drawing of an infant's shoe, half worn out, with the airy print of the blessed foot within; a thing that would make a mother smile or weep out of the very depths of her heart; and yet an actual mother would not have been likely to appreciate the poetry of the little shoe, until Miriam revealed it to her. It was wonderful, the depth and force with which the above, and other kindred subjects were depicted, and the profound significance which they often acquired. The artist, still in her fresh youth, could not probably have drawn any of these dear and rich experiences from her own life; unless, perchance, that first sketch of all, the avowal of maiden affection, were a remembered incident, and not a prophecy. But it is more delightful to believe that, from first to last, they were the productions of a beautiful imagination, dealing with the warm and pure suggestions of a woman's heart, and thus idealizing a truer and lovelier picture of the life that belongs to woman, than an actual acquaintance with some of its hard and dusty facts could have inspired. So considered, the sketches intimated such a force and variety of imaginative sympathies as would enable Miriam to fill her life richly with the bliss and suffering of womanhood, however barren it might individually be.

There was one observable point, indeed, betokening that the artist relinquished, for her personal self, the happiness which she could so profoundly appreciate for others. In all those sketches of common life, and the affections that spiritualize it, a figure was portrayed apart: now it peeped between the branches of a shrubbery, amid which two lovers sat; now it was looking through a frosted window, from the outside, while a young wedded pair sat at their new fireside, within; and once it leaned from a chariot, which six horses were whirling onward in pomp and pride, and gazed at a scene of humble enjoyment by a cottage-door. Always it was the same figure, and always depicted with an expression of deep sadness; and in every instance, slightly as they were brought out, the face and form had the traits of Miriam's own.

"Do you like these sketches better, Donatello?" asked Miriam.

"Yes," said Donatello, rather doubtfully.

"Not much, I fear," responded she, laughing. "And what should a boy like you—a Faun, too—know about the joys and sorrows, the intertwining light and shadow, of human life? I forgot that you were a Faun. You cannot suffer deeply; therefore you can but half enjoy. Here, now, is a subject which you can better appreciate."

The sketch represented merely a rustic dance, but with such extravagance of fun as was delightful to behold; and here there was no drawback, except that strange sigh and sadness which always come when we are merriest.

"I am going to paint the picture in oils," said the

artist; "and I want you, Donatello, for the wildest dancer of them all. Will you sit for me, some day?—or, rather, dance for me?"

"Oh! most gladly signorina!" exclaimed Donatello. "See; it shall be like this."

And forthwith he began to dance, and flit about the studio, like an incarnate sprite of jollity, pausing at last on the extremity of one toe, as if that were the only portion of himself, whereby his frisky nature could come in contact with the earth. The effect in that shadowy chamber, whence the artist had so carefully excluded the sunshine, was as enlivening as if one bright ray had contrived to shimmer in and frolic around the walls, and finally rest just in the centre of the floor.

"That was admirable!" said Miriam, with an approving smile. "If I can catch you on my canvas, it will be a glorious picture; only I am afraid you will dance out of it, by the very truth of the representation, just when I shall have given it the last touch. We will try it one of these days. And now, to reward you for that jolly exhibition, you shall see what has been shown to no one else."

She went to her easel, on which was placed a picture with its back turned towards the spectator. Reversing the position, there appeared the portrait of a beautiful woman, such as one sees only two or three, if even so many times, in all a lifetime; so beautiful, that she seemed to get into your consciousness and memory, and could never afterwards be shut out, but haunted your dreams, for pleasure or for pain; holding your inner realm as a conquered territory, though without deigning to make herself at home there.

She was very youthful, and had what was usually thought to be a Jewish aspect; a complexion in which there was no roseate bloom, yet neither was it pale; dark eyes, into which you might look as deeply as your glance would go, and still be conscious of a depth that you had not sounded, though it lay open to the day. She had black, abundant hair, with none of the vulgar glossiness of other women's sable locks; if she were really of Jewish blood, then this was Jewish hair, and a dark glory such as crowns no Christian maiden's head. Gazing at this portrait, you saw what Rachel might have been, when Jacob deemed her worth the wooing seven years, and seven more; or perchance she might ripen to be what Judith was, when she vanquished Holofernes with her beauty, and slew him for too much adoring it.

Miriam watched Donatello's contemplation of the picture, and seeing his simple rapture, a smile of pleasure brightened on her face, mixed with a little scorn; at least, her lips curled and her eyes gleamed, as if she disdained either his admiration or her own enjoyment of it.

"Then you like the picture, Donatello?" she asked.

"Oh, beyond what I can tell!" he answered. "So beautiful!—so beautiful!"

"And do you recognize the likeness?"

"Signorina," exclaimed Donatello, turning from the

picture to the artist, in astonishment that she should ask the question, "the resemblance is as little to be mistaken as if you had bent over the smooth surface of a fountain, and possessed the witchcraft to call forth the image that you made there! It is yourself!"

Donatello said the truth; and we forbore to speak descriptively of Miriam's beauty earlier in our narrative, because we foresaw this occasion to bring it perhaps more forcibly before the reader.

We know not whether the portrait were a flattered likeness; probably not, regarding it merely as the delineation of a lovely face; although Miriam, like all self-painters, may have endowed herself with certain graces which other eyes might not discern. Artists are fond of painting their own portraits; and, in Florence, there is a gallery of hundreds of them, including the most illustrious, in all of which there are autobiographical characteristics, so to speak; traits, expressions, loftinesses, and amenities, which would have been invisible, had they not been painted from within. Yet their reality and truth are none the less. Miriam, in like manner, had doubtless conveyed some of the intimate results of her heart-knowledge into her own portrait, and perhaps wished to try whether they would be perceptible to so simple and natural an observer as Donatello.

"Does the expression please you?" she asked.

"Yes," said Donatello, hesitatingly; "if it would only smile so like the sunshine as you sometimes do.

No, it is sadder than I thought at first. Cannot you make yourself smile a little, signorina?"

"A forced smile is uglier than a frown," said Miriam, a bright, natural smile breaking out over her face, even as she spoke.

"Oh! catch it now!" cried Donatello, clapping his hands. "Let it shine upon the picture! There! it has vanished already! And you are sad again, very sad; and the picture gazes sadly forth at me, as if some evil had befallen it in the little time since I looked last."

"How perplexed you seem, my friend!" answered Miriam. "I really half believe you are a Faun, there is such a mystery and terror for you in these dark moods, which are just as natural as daylight to us people of ordinary mould. I advise you, at all events, to look at other faces with those innocent and happy eyes, and never more to gaze at mine!"

"You speak in vain," replied the young man, with a deeper emphasis than she had ever before heard in his voice; "shroud yourself in what gloom you will, I must needs follow you."

"Well, well, well," said Miriam, impatiently: "but leave me now; for, to speak plainly, my good friend, you grow a little wearisome. I walk this afternoon in the Borghese grounds. Meet me there, if it suits your pleasure."

CHAPTER VI.

The Virgin's Shrine.

After Donatello had left the studio, Miriam herself came forth, and taking her way through some of the intricacies of the city, entered what might be called either a widening of a street, or a small piazza. The neighbourhood comprised a baker's oven, emitting the usual fragrance of sour bread; a shoe shop; a linen-draper's shop; a pipe and cigar shop; a lottery office; a station for French soldiers, with a sentinel pacing in front; and a fruit stand, at which a Roman matron was selling the dried kernels of chesnuts, wretched little figs, and some bouquets of yesterday. A church, of course, was near at hand, the façade of which ascended into lofty pinnacles, whereon were perched two or three winged figures of stone, either angelic or allegorical, blowing stone trumpets in close vicinity to the upper windows of an old and shabby palace. This palace was distinguished by a feature not very common in the architecture of Roman edifices; that is to say, a mediæval tower, square, massive, lofty, and battlemented and machicolated at the summit.

At one of the angles of the battlements stood a shrine of the Virgin, such as we see everywhere at the street-corners of Rome, but seldom or never, except in this solitary instance, at a height above the ordinary level of men's views and aspirations. Connected with this old tower and its lofty shrine, there is a legend which we cannot here pause to tell; but for centuries a lamp has been burning before the Virgin's image, at noon, at midnight, and at all hours of the twenty-four, and must be kept burning for ever, as long as the tower shall stand; or else the tower itself, the palace, and whatever estate belongs to it, shall pass from its hereditary possessor, in accordance with an ancient vow, and become the property of the Church.

As Miriam approached, she looked upward, and saw—not, indeed, the flame of the never-dying lamp, which was swallowed up in the broad sunlight that brightened the shrine—but a flock of white doves, skimming, fluttering, and wheeling about the topmost height of the tower, their silver wings flashing in the pure transparency of the air. Several of them sat on the ledge of the upper window, pushing one another off by their eager struggle for this favourite station, and all tapping their beaks and flapping their wings tumultuously against the panes; some had alighted in the street, far below, but flew hastily upward, at the sound of the window being thrust ajar, and opening in the middle, on rusty hinges, as Roman windows do.

A fair young girl, dressed in white, showed herself at the aperture for a single instant, and threw forth as much as her two small hands could hold of some kind of food, for the flock of eleemosynary doves. It seemed greatly to the taste of the feathered people; for they tried to snatch beakfuls of it from her grasp, caught it in the air, and rushed downward after it upon the pavement.

"What a pretty scene this is," thought Miriam, with a kindly smile, "and how like a dove she is herself, the fair, pure creature! The other doves know her for a sister, I am sure."

Miriam passed beneath the deep portal of the palace, and turning to the left, began to mount flight after flight of a staircase, which, for the loftiness of its aspiration, was worthy to be Jacob's ladder, or, at all events, the staircase of the Tower of Babel. The city bustle, which is heard even in Rome, the rumble of wheels over the uncomfortable paving-stones, the hard harsh cries, re-echoing in the high and narrow streets, grew faint and died away; as the turmoil of the world will always die, if we set our faces to climb heavenward. Higher, and higher still; and now, glancing through the successive windows that threw in their narrow light upon the stairs, her view stretched across the roofs of the city, unimpeded even by the stateliest palaces. Only the domes of churches ascend into this airy region, and hold up their golden crosses on a level with her eye; except that, out of the very heart of Rome, the column of Antoninus thrusts itself upward, with St. Paul upon its summit, the sole human form that seems to have kept her company.

Finally, the staircase came to an end; save that, on one side of the little entry where it terminated, a flight of a dozen steps gave access to the roof of the tower and the legendary shrine. On the other side was a door, at which Miriam knocked, but rather as a friendly announcement of her presence than with any doubt of hospitable welcome; for, awaiting no response, she lifted the latch and entered.

"What a hermitage you have found for yourself, dear Hilda!" she exclaimed. "You breathe sweet air, above all the evil scents of Rome; and even so, in your maiden elevation, you dwell above our vanities and passions, our moral dust and mud, with the doves and the angels for your nearest neighbours. I should not wonder if the Catholics were to make a saint of you, like your namesake of old; especially as you have almost avowed yourself of their religion, by undertaking to keep the lamp alight before the Virgin's shrine."

"No, no, Miriam!" said Hilda, who had come joyfully forward to greet her friend. "You must not call me a Catholic. A Christian girl—even a daughter of the Puritans—may surely pay honour to the idea of divine Womanhood, without giving up the faith of her forefathers. But how kind you are to climb into my dovecote!"

"It is no trifling proof of friendship, indeed," answered Miriam; "I should think there were three hundred stairs at least."

"But it will do you good," continued Hilda. "A height of some fifty feet above the roofs of Rome gives me all the advantages that I could get from fifty miles of distance. The air so exhilarates my spirits, that sometimes I feel half inclined to attempt a flight from the top of my tower, in the faith that I should float upward."

"Oh, pray don't try it!" said Miriam, laughing. "If it should turn out that you are less than an angel, you would find the stones of the Roman pavement very hard; and if an angel, indeed, I am afraid you would never come down among us again."

This young American girl was an example of the freedom of life which it is possible for a female artist to enjoy at Rome. She dwelt in her tower, as free to descend into the corrupted atmosphere of the city beneath, as one of her companion doves to fly downward into the street;—all alone, perfectly independent, under her own sole guardianship, unless watched over by the Virgin, whose shrine she tended; doing what she liked, without a suspicion or a shadow upon the snowy whiteness of her fame. The customs of artist life bestow such liberty upon the sex, which is elsewhere restricted within so much narrower limits; and it is perhaps an indication that, whenever we admit women to a wider scope of pursuits and professions, we must also remove the shackles of our present conventional rules, which would then become an insufferable restraint on either maid or wife. The system seems to work unexceptionably in Rome; and in many other cases, as in Hilda's, purity of heart and life are allowed to assert themselves, and to be their own proof and security, to a degree unknown in the society of other cities.

Hilda, in her native land, had early shown what

was pronounced by connoisseurs a decided genius for the pictorial art. Even in her school days—still not so very distant—she had produced sketches that were seized upon by men of taste, and hoarded as among the choicest treasures of their portfolios; scenes delicately imagined, lacking, perhaps, the reality which comes only from a close acquaintance with life, but so softly touched with feeling and fancy that you seemed to be looking at humanity with angels' eyes. With years and experience she might be expected to attain a darker and more forcible touch, which would impart to her designs the relief they needed. Had Hilda remained in her own country it is not improbable that she might have produced original works worthy to hang in that gallery of native art which, we hope, is destined to extend its rich length through many future centuries. An orphan, however, without near relatives, and possessed of a little property, she had found it within her possibilities to come to Italy; that central clime, whither the eyes and the heart of every artist turn, as if pictures could not be made to glow in any other atmosphere, as if statues could not assume grace and expression save in that land of whitest marble.

Hilda's gentle courage had brought her safely over land and sea; her mild, unflagging perseverance had made a place for her in the famous city, even like a flower that finds a chink for itself, and a little earth to grow in, on whatever ancient wall its slender roots may fasten. Here she dwelt, in her tower, possessing a friend or two in Rome, but no home companion except the flock of doves, whose cote was in a ruinous chamber contiguous to her own. They soon became as familiar with the fair-haired Saxon girl as if she were a born sister of their brood; and her customary white robe bore such an analogy to their snowy plumage that the confraternity of artists called Hilda the Dove, and recognized her aërial apartment as the Dovecote. And while the other doves flew far and wide in quest of what was good for them, Hilda likewise spread her wings, and sought such ethereal and imaginative sustenance as God ordains for creatures of her kind.

We know not whether the result of her Italian studies, so far as it could yet be seen, will be accepted as a good or desirable one. Certain it is, that, since her arrival in the pictorial land, Hilda seemed to have entirely lost the impulse of original design, which brought her thither. No doubt the girl's early dreams had been of sending forms and hues of beauty into the visible world out of her own mind; of compelling scenes of poetry and history to live before men's eyes, through conceptions and by methods individual to herself. But more and more, as she grew familiar with the miracles of art that enrich so many galleries in Rome, Hilda had ceased to consider herself as an original artist. No wonder that this change should have befallen her. She was endowed with a deep and sensitive faculty of appreciation; she had the gift of discerning and worshipping excellence in a most unusual measure. No other person, it is probable, recognized so adequately, and enjoyed with such deep delight, the pictorial wonders that were here displayed. She saw — no, not saw, but felt — through and through a picture; she bestowed upon it all the warmth and richness of a woman's sympathy; not by any intellectual effort, but by this strength of heart, and this guiding light of sympathy, she went straight to the central point, in which the master had conceived his work. Thus, she viewed it, as it were, with his own eyes, and hence her comprehension of any picture that interested her was perfect.

This power and depth of appreciation depended partly upon Hilda's physical organization, which was at once healthful and exquisitely delicate; and, connected with this advantage, she had a command of hand, a nicety and force of touch, which is an endowment separate from pictorial genius, though indispensable to its exercise.

It has probably happened in many other instances, as it did in Hilda's case, that she ceased to aim at original achievement in consequence of the very gifts which so exquisitely fitted her to profit by familiarity with the works of the mighty old masters. Reverencing these wonderful men so deeply, she was too grateful for all they bestowed upon her, too loyal, too humble, in their awful presence, to think of enrolling herself in their society. Beholding the miracles of beauty which they had achieved, the world seemed already rich enough in original designs, and nothing more was so desirable as to diffuse those selfsame beauties more widely among mankind. All the youthful hopes and ambitions, the fanciful ideas which she had brought from home, of great pictures to be conceived in her feminine mind, were flung aside, and, so far as those most intimate with her could discern, relinquished without a sigh. All that she would henceforth attempt —and that most reverently, not to say religiously—was to catch and reflect some of the glory which had been shed upon canvas from the immortal pencils of old.

So Hilda became a copyist: in the Pinacotheca of the Vatican, in the galleries of the Pamfili-Doria palace, the Borghese, the Corsini, the Sciarra, her easel was set up before many a famous picture of Guido, Domenichino, Raphael, and the devout painters of earlier schools than these. Other artists and visitors from foreign lands beheld the slender, girlish figure in front of some world-known work, absorbed, unconscious of everything around her, seeming to live only in what she sought to do. They smiled, no doubt, at the audacity which led her to dream of copying those mighty achievements. But, if they paused to look over her shoulder, and had sensibility enough to understand what was before their eyes, they soon felt inclined to believe that the spirits of the old masters were hovering over Hilda, and guiding her delicate white hand. In truth, from whatever realm of bliss and many-coloured beauty those spirits might descend, it would have been no unworthy errand to help so gentle and pure a worshipper of their genius in giving the last divine touch to her repetitions of their works.

Her copies were indeed marvellous. Accuracy was

not the phrase for them; a Chinese copy is accurate. Hilda's had that evanescent and ethereal life—that flitting fragrance, as it were, of the originals—which it is as difficult to catch and retain as it would be for a sculptor to get the very movement and varying colour of a living man into his marble bust. Only by watching the efforts of the most skilful copyists—men who spend a lifetime, as some of them do, in multiplying copies of a single picture—and observing how invariably they leave out just the indefinable charm that involves the last, inestimable value, can we understand the difficulties of the task which they undertake.

It was not Hilda's general practice to attempt reproducing the whole of a great picture, but to select some high, noble, and delicate portion of it, in which the spirit and essence of the picture culminated: the Virgin's celestial sorrow, for example, or a hovering angel, imbued with immortal light, or a saint with the glow of heaven in his dying face—and these would be rendered with her whole soul. If a picture had darkened into an indistinct shadow through time and neglect, or had been injured by cleaning, or retouched by some profane hand, she seemed to possess the faculty of seeing it in its pristine glory. The copy would come from her hands with what the beholder felt must be the light which the old master had left upon the original in bestowing his final and most ethereal touch. In some instances even (at least, so those believed who best appreciated Hilda's power and sensibility), she had been enabled to execute what the great master had conceived in his imagination, but had not so perfectly succeeded in putting upon canvas; a result surely not impossible when such depth of sympathy as she possessed was assisted by the delicate skill and accuracy of her slender hand. In such cases the girl was but a finer instrument, a more exquisitely effective piece of mechanism, by the help of which the spirit of some great departed painter now first achieved his ideal, centuries after his own earthly hand, that other tool, had turned to dust.

Not to describe her as too much a wonder, however, Hilda, or the Dove, as her well-wishers half laughingly delighted to call her, had been pronounced by good judges incomparably the best copyist in Rome. After minute examination of her works, the most skilful artists declared that she had been led to her results by following precisely the same process step by step through which the original painter had trodden to the development of his idea. Other copyists—if such they are worthy to be called—attempt only a superficial imitation. Copies of the old masters in this sense are produced by thousands; there are artists, as we have said, who spend their lives in painting the works, or perhaps one single work of one illustrious painter over and over again: thus they convert themselves into Guido machines, or Raphaelic machines. Their performances, it is true, are often wonderfully deceptive to a careless eye; but working entirely from the outside, and seeking only to reproduce the surface, these men are sure to leave out that indefinable nothing, that inestimable something, that constitutes the life and soul through which the picture gets its immortality. Hilda was no such machine as this; she wrought religiously, and therefore wrought a miracle.

It strikes us that there is something far higher and nobler in all this, in her thus sacrificing herself to the devout recognition of the highest excellence in art, than there would have been in cultivating her not inconsiderable share of talent for the production of works from her own ideas. She might have set up for herself, and won no ignoble name; she might have helped to fill the already crowded and cumbered world with pictures, not destitute of merit, but falling short, if by ever so little, of the best that has been done; she might thus have gratified some tastes that were incapable of appreciating Raphael. But this could be done only by lowering the standard of art to the comprehension of the spectator. She chose the better, and loftier, and more unselfish part, laying her individual hopes, her fame, her prospects of enduring remembrance, at the feet of those great departed ones, whom she so loved and venerated; and therefore the world was the richer for this feeble girl.

Since the beauty and glory of a great picture are confined within itself, she won out that glory by patient faith and self-devotion, and multiplied it for mankind. From the dark, chill corner of a gallery—from some curtained chapel in a church, where the light came seldom and aslant—from the prince's carefully guarded cabinet, where not one eye in thousands was permitted to behold it — she brought the wondrous picture into daylight, and gave all its magic splendour for the enjoyment of the world. Hilda's faculty of genuine admiration is one of the rarest to be found in human nature; and let us try to recompense her in kind by admiring her generous self-surrender, and her brave, humble magnanimity in choosing to be the handmaid of those old magicians, instead of a minor enchantress within a circle of her own.

The handmaid of Raphael, whom she loved with a virgin's love! Would it have been worth Hilda's while to relinquish this office for the sake of giving the world a picture or two which it would call original; pretty fancies of snow and moonlight; the counterpart in picture of so many feminine achievements in literature!

CHAPTER VII.

Beatrice.

Miriam was glad to find the Dove in her turret-home; for being endowed with an infinite activity, and taking exquisite delight in the sweet labour of which her life was full, it was Hilda's practice to flee abroad betimes and haunt the galleries till dusk. Happy were those (but they were very few) whom she ever chose to be the companions of her day; they saw the art-treasures of Rome, under her guidance, as they had never seen them before. Not that Hilda could dissertate, or talk learnedly about pictures; she would probably have been puzzled by the technical terms of her own art. Not that she had much to say about what she most profoundly admired; but even her silent sympathy was so powerful that it drew your own along with it, endowing you with a second-sight that enabled you to see excellences with almost the depth and delicacy of her own perceptions.

All the Anglo-Saxon denizens of Rome, by this time, knew Hilda by sight. Unconsciously, the poor child had become one of the spectacles of the Eternal City, and was often pointed out to strangers, sitting at her easel among the wild-bearded young men, the white-haired old ones, and the shabbily dressed, painfully plain women, who make up the throng of copyists. The old custodes knew her well, and watched over her as their own child. Sometimes a young artist, instead of going on with a copy of the picture before which he had placed his easel, would enrich his canvas with an original portrait of Hilda at her work. A lovelier subject could not have been selected, nor one which required nicer skill and insight in doing it anything like justice. She was pretty at all times, in our native New England style, with her light-brown ringlets, her delicately tinged, but healthful cheek, her sensitive, intelligent, yet most feminine and kindly face. But, every few moments, this pretty and girlish face grew beautiful and striking, as some inward thought and feeling brightened, rose to the surface, and then, as it were, passed out of sight again; so that, taking into view this constantly recurring change, it really seemed as if Hilda were only visible by the sunshine of her soul.

In other respects, she was a good subject for a portrait, being distinguished by a gentle picturesqueness, which was perhaps unconsciously bestowed by some minute peculiarity of dress, such as artists seldom fail to assume. The effect was to make her appear like an inhabitant of picture-land, a partly ideal creature, not to be handled, nor even approached too closely. In her feminine self, Hilda was natural, and of pleasant deportment, endowed with a mild cheerfulness of temper, not overflowing with animal spirits, but never long despondent. There was a certain simplicity that made every one her friend, but it was combined with a subtle attribute of reserve, that insensibly kept those at a distance who were not suited to her sphere.

Miriam was the dearest friend whom she had ever known. Being a year or two the elder, of longer acquaintance with Italy, and better fitted to deal with its crafty and selfish inhabitants, she had helped Hilda to arrange her way of life, and had encouraged her through those first weeks, when Rome is so dreary to every new-comer.

"But how lucky that you are at home to-day," said Miriam, continuing the conversation which was begun, many pages back. "I hardly hoped to find you, though I had a favour to ask—a commission to put into your charge. But what picture is this?"

"See!" said Hilda, taking her friend's hand and leading her in front of the easel. "I wanted your opinion of it."

"If you have really succeeded," observed Miriam, recognizing the picture at the first glance, "it will be the greatest miracle you have yet achieved."

The picture represented simply a female head; a very youthful, girlish, perfectly beautiful face, enveloped in white drapery, from beneath which strayed a lock or two of what seemed a rich, though hidden luxuriance of auburn hair. The eyes were large and brown, and met those of the spectator, but evidently with a strange, ineffectual effort to escape. There was a little redness about the eyes, very slightly indicated, so that you would question whether or no the girl had been

weeping. The whole face was quiet; there was no distortion or disturbance of any single feature; nor was it easy to see why the expression was not cheerful, or why a single touch of the artist's pencil should not brighten it into joyousness. But, in fact, it was the very saddest picture ever painted or conceived; it involved an unfathomable depth of sorrow, the sense of which came to the observer by a sort of intuition. It was a sorrow that removed this beautiful girl out of the sphere of humanity, and set her in a far-off region, the remoteness of which—while yet her face is so close before us—makes us shiver as at a spectre.

"Yes, Hilda," said her friend, after closely examining the picture, "you have done nothing else so wonderful as this. But by what unheard-of solicitations or secret interest have you obtained leave to copy Guido's Beatrice Cenci? It is an unexampled favour; and the impossibility of getting a genuine copy has filled the Roman picture-shops with Beatrices, gay, grievous, or coquettish, but never a true one among them."

"There has been one exquisite copy, I have heard," said Hilda, "by an artist capable of appreciating the spirit of the picture. It was Thompson, who brought it away piecemeal, being forbidden (like the rest of us) to set up his easel before it. As for me, I knew the Prince Barberini would be deaf to all entreaties; so I had no resource but to sit down before the picture, day after day, and let it sink into my heart. I do believe it is now photographed there. It is a sad face to keep so close to one's heart; only, what is so very beautiful can never be quite a pain. Well; after studying it in this way, I know not how many times, I came home, and have done my best to transfer the image to canvas."

"Here it is then," said Miriam, contemplating Hilda's work with great interest and delight, mixed with the painful sympathy that the picture excited. "Everywhere we see oil-paintings, crayon sketches, cameos, engravings, lithographs, pretending to be Beatrice, and representing the poor girl with blubbered eyes, a leer of coquetry, a merry look as if she were dancing, a piteous look as if she were beaten, and twenty other modes of fantastic mistake. But here is Guido's very Beatrice; she that slept in the dungeon, and awoke betimes, to ascend the scaffold. And now that you have done it, Hilda, can you interpret what the feeling is, that gives this picture such a mysterious force? For my part, though deeply sensible of its influence, I cannot seize it."

"Nor can I, in words," replied her friend. "But while I was painting her, I felt all the time as if she were trying to escape from my gaze. She knows that her sorrow is so strange and so immense, that she ought to be solitary for ever, both for the world's sake and her own; and this is the reason we feel such a distance between Beatrice and ourselves, even when our eyes meet hers. It is infinitely heart-breaking to meet her glance, and to feel that nothing can be done to help or comfort her; neither does she ask help or comfort, knowing the hopelessness of her case better than we do.

She is a fallen angel—fallen, and yet sinless; and it is only this depth of sorrow, with its weight and darkness, that keeps her down upon earth, and brings her within our view even while it sets her beyond our reach."

"You deem her sinless?" asked Miriam; "that is not so plain to me. If I can pretend to see at all into that dim region, whence she gazes so strangely and sadly at us, Beatrice's own conscience does not acquit her of something evil, and never to be forgiven!"

"Sorrow so black as hers oppresses her very nearly as sin would," said Hilda.

"Then," inquired Miriam, "do you think that there was no sin in the deed for which she suffered?"

"Ah!" replied Hilda, shuddering, "I really had quite forgotten Beatrice's history, and was thinking of her only as the picture seems to reveal her character. Yes, yes; it was terrible guilt, an inexpiable crime, and she feels it to be so. Therefore it is that the forlorn creature so longs to elude our eyes, and for ever vanish away into nothingness! Her doom is just!"

"Oh! Hilda, your innocence is like a sharp steel sword," exclaimed her friend. "Your judgments are often terribly severe, though you seem all made up of gentleness and mercy. Beatrice's sin may not have been so great: perhaps it was no sin at all, but the best virtue possible in the circumstances. If she viewed it as a sin, it may have been because her nature was too feeble for the fate imposed upon her. Ah!" continued Miriam, passionately, "if I could only get within her consciousness! — if I could but clasp Beatrice Cenci's ghost, and draw it into myself! I would give my life to know whether she thought herself innocent, or the one great criminal since time began."

As Miriam gave utterance to these words, Hilda looked from the picture into her face, and was startled to observe that her friend's expression had become almost exactly that of the portrait; as if her passionate wish and struggle to penetrate poor Beatrice's mystery had been successful.

"Oh! for Heaven's sake, Miriam, do not look so!" she cried. "What an actress you are! And I never guessed it before. Ah! now you are yourself again!" she added, kissing her. "Leave Beatrice to me in future."

"Cover up your magical picture, then," replied her friend, "else I never can look away from it. It is strange, dear Hilda, how an innocent, delicate, white soul like yours has been able to seize the subtle mystery of this portrait; as you surely must, in order to reproduce it so perfectly. Well; we will not talk of it any more. Do you know, I have come to you this morning on a small matter of business. Will you undertake it for me?"

"Oh, certainly," said Hilda, laughing; "if you choose to trust me with business."

"Nay, it is not a matter of any difficulty," answered Miriam; "merely to take charge of this pacquet, and keep it for me awhile."

"But why not keep it yourself?" asked Hilda.

"Partly because it will be safer in your charge," said her friend. "I am a careless sort of person in ordinary things; while you, for all you dwell so high above the world, have certain good little housewifely ways of accuracy and order. The pacquet is of some slight importance; and yet, it may be, I shall not ask you for it again. In a week or two, you know, I am leaving Rome. You, setting at defiance the malaria fever, mean to stay here and haunt your beloved galleries through the summer. Now, four months hence, unless you hear more from me, I would have you deliver the pacquet according to its address."

Hilda read the direction: it was to Signore Luca Barboni, at the Palazzo Cenci, third piano.

"I will deliver it with my own hand," said she, "precisely four months from to-day, unless you bid me to the contrary. Perhaps I shall meet the ghost of Beatrice in that grim old palace of her forefathers."

"In that case," rejoined Miriam, "do not fail to speak to her, and try to win her confidence. Poor thing! she would be all the better for pouring her heart out freely, and would be glad to do it, if she were sure of sympathy. It irks my brain and heart to think of her, all shut up within herself." She withdrew the cloth that Hilda had drawn over the picture, and took another long look at it—"Poor sister Beatrice! for she was still a woman, Hilda, still a sister, be her sin or sorrow what they might. How well you have done it, Hilda! I know not whether Guido will thank you, or be jealous of your rivalship."

"Jealous, indeed!" exclaimed Hilda. "If Guido had not wrought through me, my pains would have been thrown away."

"After all," resumed Miriam, "if a woman had painted the original picture, there might have been something in it which we miss now. I have a great mind to undertake a copy myself, and try to give it what it lacks. Well; good bye. But, stay! I am going for a little airing to the grounds of the Villa Borghese this afternoon. You will think it very foolish, but I always feel the safer in your company, Hilda, slender little maiden as you are. Will you come?"

"Ah, not to-day, dearest Miriam," she replied, "I have set my heart on giving another touch or two to this picture, and shall not stir abroad till nearly sunset."

"Farewell, then," said her visitor. "I leave you in your dovecote. What a sweet, strange life you lead here; conversing with the souls of the old masters, feeding and fondling your sister doves, and trimming the Virgin's lamp! Hilda, do you ever pray to the Virgin while you tend her shrine?"

"Sometimes I have been moved to do so," replied the Dove, blushing and lowering her eyes; "she was a woman once. Do you think it would be wrong?"

"Nay, that is for you to judge," said Miriam; "but when you pray next, dear friend, remember me!"

She went down the long descent of the lower staircase, and just as she reached the street the flock of doves again took their hurried flight from the pavement to the topmost window. She threw her eyes upward and beheld them hovering about Hilda's head; for after her friend's departure the girl had been more impressed than before by something very sad and troubled in her manner. She was, therefore, leaning forth from her airy abode, and flinging down a kind, maidenly kiss, and a gesture of farewell, in the hope that these might alight upon Miriam's heart and comfort its unknown sorrow a little. Kenyon the sculptor, who chanced to be passing the head of the street, took note of that ethereal kiss, and wished that he could have caught it in the air and got Hilda's leave to keep it.

CHAPTER VIII.

The Suburban Villa.

DONATELLO, while it was still a doubtful question betwixt afternoon and morning, set forth to keep the appointment which Miriam had carelessly tendered him in the grounds of the Villa Borghese.

The entrance to these grounds (as all my readers know, for everybody now-a-days has been in Rome) is just outside of the Porta del Popolo. Passing beneath that not very impressive specimen of Michael Angelo's architecture, a minute's walk will transport the visitor from the small, uneasy lava stones of the Roman pavement into broad, gravelled carriage-drives, whence a little farther stroll brings him to the soft turf of a beautiful seclusion. A seclusion, but seldom a solitude; for priest, noble and populace, stranger and native, all who breathe Roman air, find free admission, and come hither to taste the languid enjoyment of the day-dream that they call life.

But Donatello's enjoyment was of a livelier kind. He soon began to draw long and delightful breaths among those shadowy walks. Judging by the pleasure which the sylvan character of the scene excited in him, it might be no merely fanciful theory to set him down as the kinsman, not far remote, of that wild, sweet,

playful, rustic creature, to whose marble image he bore so striking a resemblance. How mirthful a discovery would it be (and yet with a touch of pathos in it), if the breeze which sported fondly with his clustering locks were to waft them suddenly aside, and show a pair of leaf-shaped, furry ears! What an honest strain of wildness would it indicate! and into what regions of rich mystery would it extend Donatello's sympathies, to be thus linked (and by no monstrous chain) with what we call the inferior tribes of being, whose simplicity, mingled with his human intelligence, might partly restore what man has lost of the divine!

The scenery amid which the youth now strayed was such as arrays itself in the imagination when we read the beautiful old myths, and fancy a brighter sky, a softer turf, a more picturesque arrangement of venerable trees, than we find in the rude and untrained landscapes of the Western world. The ilex-trees, so ancient and time-honoured were they, seemed to have lived for ages undisturbed, and to feel no dread of profanation by the axe any more than overthrow by the thunder-stroke. It had already passed out of their dreamy old memories that only a few years ago they were grievously imperilled by the Gaul's last assault upon the walls of Rome. As if confident in the long peace of their lifetime, they assumed attitudes of indolent repose. They leaned over the green turf in ponderous grace, throwing abroad their great branches without danger of interfering with other trees, though other majestic trees grew near enough for dignified society, but too distant for constraint. Never was there a more venerable quietude than that which slept among their sheltering boughs; never a sweeter sunshine than that now gladdening the gentle gloom which these leafy patriarchs strove to diffuse over the swelling and subsiding lawns.

In other portions of the grounds the stone-pines lifted their dense clump of branches upon a slender length of stem, so high that they looked like green islands in the air, flinging down a shadow upon the turf so far off that you hardly knew which tree had made it. Again, there were avenues of cypress, resembling dark flames of huge funeral candles, which spread dusk and twilight round about them instead of cheerful radiance. The more open spots were all abloom, even so early in the season, with anemones of wondrous size, both white and rose-coloured, and violets that betrayed themselves by their rich fragrance, even if their blue eyes failed to meet your own. Daisies, too, were abundant, but larger than the modest little English flower, and therefore of small account.

These wooded and flowery lawns are more beautiful than the finest of English park-scenery, more touching, more impressive, through the neglect that leaves nature so much to her own ways and methods. Since man seldom interferes with her, she sets to work in her quiet way and makes herself at home. There is enough of human care, it is true, bestowed long ago and still bestowed, to prevent wildness from growing into deformity; and the result is an ideal landscape, a woodland scene that seems to have been projected out of the poet's mind. If the ancient Faun were other than a mere creation of old poetry, and could have reappeared anywhere, it must have been in such a scene as this.

In the openings of the wood there are fountains plashing into marble basins, the depths of which are shaggy with water-weeds; or they tumble like natural cascades from rock to rock, sending their murmur afar, to make the quiet and silence more appreciable. Scattered here and there with careless artifice, stand old altars bearing Roman inscriptions. Statues, gray with the long corrosion of even that soft atmosphere half hide and half reveal themselves, high on pedestals, or perhaps fallen and broken on the turf. Terminal figures, columns of marble or granite porticoes, arches, are seen in the vistas of the wood-paths, either veritable relics of antiquity, or with so exquisite a touch of artful ruin on them that they are better than if really antique. At all events, grass grows on the tops of the shattered pillars, and weeds and flowers root themselves in the chinks of the massive arches and fronts of temples, and clamber at large over their pediments, as if this were the thousandth summer since their winged seeds alighted there.

What a strange idea—what a needless labour—to construct artificial ruins in Rome, the native soil of ruin? But even these sportive imitations, wrought by man in emulation of what time has done to temples and palaces, are perhaps centuries old, and, beginning as illusions, have grown to be venerable in sober earnest. The result of all is a scene, pensive, lovely, dream-like, enjoyable and sad, such as is to be found nowhere save in these princely villa-residences in the neighbourhood of Rome; a scene that must have required generations and ages, during which growth, decay, and man's intelligence wrought kindly together, to render it so gently wild as we behold it now.

The final charm is bestowed by the malaria. There is a piercing, thrilling, delicious kind of regret in the idea of so much beauty thrown away, or only enjoyable at its half-development, in winter and early spring, and never to be dwelt amongst, as the home-scenery of any human being. For if you come hither in summer, and stray through these glades in the golden sunset, fever walks arm in arm with you, and death awaits you at the end of the dim vista. Thus the scene is like Eden in its loveliness; like Eden, too, in the fatal spell that removes it beyond the scope of man's actual possessions. But Donatello felt nothing of this dream-like melancholy that haunts the spot. As he passed among the sunny shadows, his spirit seemed to acquire new elasticity. The flicker of the sunshine, the sparkle of the fountain's gush, the dance of the leaf upon the bough, the woodland fragrance, the green freshness, the old sylvan peace and freedom, were all intermingled in those long breaths which he drew.

The ancient dust, the mouldiness of Rome, the dead atmosphere in which he had wasted so many months, the hard pavements, the smell of ruin and decaying generations, the chill palaces, the convent-bells, the heavy incense of altars, the life that he had led in those dark, narrow streets, among priests, soldiers, nobles, artists, and women; all the sense of these things rose from the young man's consciousness like a cloud which had darkened over him without his knowing how densely.

He drank in the natural influences of the scene, and was intoxicated as by an exhilarating wine. He ran races with himself along the gleam and shadow of the wood-paths. He leapt up to catch the overhanging bough of an ilex, and swinging himself by it alighted far onward, as if he had flown thither through the air. In a sudden rapture he embraced the trunk of a sturdy tree, and seemed to imagine it a creature worthy of affection and capable of a tender response; he clasped it closely in his arms, as a Faun might have clasped the warm, feminine grace of the nymph, whom antiquity supposed to dwell within that rough, encircling rind. Then, in order to bring himself closer to the genial earth, with which his kindred instincts linked him so strongly, he threw himself at full length on the turf, and pressed down his lips, kissing the violets and daisies, which kissed him back again, though shyly, in their maiden fashion.

While he lay there, it was pleasant to see how the green and blue lizards, who had been basking on some rock or on a fallen pillar that absorbed the warmth of the sun, scrupled not to scramble over him with their small feet; and how the birds alighted on the nearest twigs and sang their little roundelays unbroken by any chirrup of alarm; they recognized him, it may be, as something akin to themselves, or else they fancied that he was rooted and grew there; for these wild pets of nature dreaded him no more in his buoyant life than if a mound of soil and grass and flowers had long since covered his dead body, converting it back to the sympathies from which human existence had estranged it.

All of us, after long abode in cities, have felt the blood gush more joyously through our veins with the first breath of rural air; few could feel it so much as Donatello, a creature of simple elements, bred in the sweet sylvan life of Tuscany, and for months back dwelling amid the mouldy gloom and dim splendour of old Rome. Nature has been shut out for numberless centuries from those stony-hearted streets, to which he had latterly grown accustomed; there is no trace of her, except for what blades of grass spring out of the pavements of the less trodden piazzas, or what weeds cluster and tuft themselves on the cornices of ruins. Therefore his joy was like that of a child that had gone astray from home, and finds him suddenly in his mother's arms again.

At last, deeming it full time for Miriam to keep her tryst, he climbed to the tiptop of the tallest tree, and thence looked about him, swaying to and fro in the gentle breeze, which was like the respiration of that great leafy, living thing. Donatello saw beneath him the whole circuit of the enchanted ground; the statues and columns pointing upward from among the shrubbery, the fountains flashing in the sunlight, the paths winding hither and thither, and continually finding out some nook of new and ancient pleasantness He saw the villa, too, with its marble front incrusted all over with bas-reliefs, and statues in its many niches. It was as beautiful as a fairy palace, and seemed an abode in which the lord and lady of this fair domain might fitly dwell, and come forth each morning to enjoy as sweet a life as their happiest dreams of the past night could have depicted. All this he saw, but his first glance had taken in too wide a sweep, and it was not till his eyes fell almost directly beneath him, that Donatello beheld Miriam just turning into the path that led across the roots of his very tree.

He descended among the foliage, waiting for her to come close to the trunk, and then suddenly dropt from an impending bough, and alighted at her side. It was as if the swaying of the branches had let a ray of sunlight through. The same ray likewise glimmered among the gloomy meditations that encompassed Miriam, and lit up the pale dark beauty of her face, while it responded pleasantly to Donatello's glance.

"I hardly know," said she, smiling, "whether you have sprouted out of the earth, or fallen from the clouds. In either case, you are welcome."

And they walked onward together.

CHAPTER IX.

The Faun and Nymph.

Miriam's sadder mood, it might be, had at first an effect on Donatello's spirits. It checked the joyous ebullition into which they would otherwise have effervesced when he found himself in her society, not, as heretofore, in the old gloom of Rome, but under that bright soft sky and in those Arcadian woods. He was silent for awhile; it being, indeed, seldom Donatello's impulse to express himself copiously in words. His usual modes of demonstration were by the natural language of gesture, the instinctive movement of his agile frame, and the unconscious play of his features, which, within a limited range of thought and emotion, would speak volumes in a moment.

By-and-by, his own mood seemed to brighten Miriam's, and was reflected back upon himself. He began inevitably, as it were, to dance along the woodpath, flinging himself into attitudes of strange comic grace. Often, too, he ran a little way in advance of his companion, and then stood to watch her as she approached along the shadowy and sun-fleckered path. With every step she took, he expressed his joy at her nearer and nearer presence by what might be thought an extravagance of gesticulation, but which doubtless was the language of the natural man, though laid aside and forgotten by other men, now that words have been feebly substituted in the place of signs and symbols. He gave Miriam the idea of a being not precisely man, nor yet a child, but, in a high and beautiful sense, an animal—a creature in a state of development less than what mankind has attained, yet the more perfect within itself for that very deficiency. This idea filled her mobile imagination with agreeable fantasies, which, after smiling at them herself, she tried to convey to the young man.

"What are you, my friend?" she exclaimed, always keeping in mind his singular resemblance to the Faun of the Capitol. "If you are, in good truth, that wild and pleasant creature whose face you wear, pray make me known to your kindred. They will be found hereabouts, if anywhere. Knock at the rough rind of this ilex-tree, and summon forth the Dryad! Ask the water-nymph to rise dripping from yonder fountain, and exchange a moist pressure of the hand with me! Do not fear that I shall shrink, even if one of your rough cousins, a hairy Satyr, should come capering on his goat-legs out of the haunts of far antiquity, and propose to dance with me among these lawns! And will not Bacchus—with whom you consorted so familiarly of old, and who loved you so well—will he not meet us here, and squeeze rich grapes into his cup for you and me?"

Donatello smiled: he laughed heartily, indeed, in sympathy with the mirth that gleamed out of Miriam's deep dark eyes. But he did not seem quite to understand her mirthful talk, nor to be disposed to explain what kind of creature he was, or to inquire with what divine or poetic kindred his companion feigned to link him. He appeared only to know that Miriam was beautiful, and that she smiled graciously upon him; that the present moment was very sweet, and himself most happy with the sunshine, the sylvan scenery, and woman's kindly charm, which it enclosed within its small circumference. It was delightful to see the trust which he reposed in Miriam, and his pure joy in her propinquity; he asked nothing, sought nothing, save to be near the beloved object, and brimmed over with ecstacy at that simple boon. A creature of the happy tribes below us sometimes shows the capacity of this enjoyment; a man, seldom or never.

"Donatello," said Miriam, looking at him thoughtfully, but amused, yet not without a shade of sorrow, "you seem very happy; what makes you so?"

"Because I love you!" answered Donatello.

He made this momentous confession as if it were the most natural thing in the world; and, on her part —such was the contagion of his simplicity—Miriam heard it without anger or disturbance, though with no responding emotion. It was as if they had strayed across the limits of Arcadia, and come under a civil polity where young men might avow their passion with as little restraint as a bird pipes its notes to a similar purpose.

"Why should you love me, foolish boy?" said she.

"We have no points of sympathy at all. There are not two creatures more unlike, in this wide world, than you and I!"

"You are yourself, and I am Donatello," replied he. "Therefore I love you! There needs no other reason."

Certainly, there was no better or more explicable reason. It might have been imagined that Donatello's unsophisticated heart would be more readily attracted to a feminine nature of clear simplicity like his own, than to one already turbid with grief or wrong, as Miriam's seemed to be. Perhaps, on the other hand, his character needed the dark element, which it found in her. The force and energy of will, that sometimes flashed through her eyes, may have taken him captive; or, not improbably, the varying lights and shadows of her temper, now so mirthful, and anon so sad with mysterious gloom, had bewitched the youth. Analyze the matter as we may, the reason assigned by Donatello himself was as satisfactory as we are likely to attain.

Miriam could not think seriously of the avowal that had passed. He held out his love so freely, in his open palm, that she felt it could be nothing but a toy, which she might play with for an instant, and give back again. And yet Donatello's heart was so fresh a fountain, that, had Miriam been more world-worn than she was, she might have found it exquisite to slake her thirst with the feelings that welled up and brimmed over from it. She was far, very far, from the dusty mediæval epoch, when some women have a taste for such refreshment. Even for her, however, there was an inexpressible charm, in the simplicity that prompted Donatello's words and deeds; though, unless she caught them in precisely the true light, they seemed but folly, the offspring of a maimed or imperfectly developed intellect. Alternately, she almost admired, or wholly scorned him, and knew not which estimate resulted from the deeper appreciation. But it could not, she decided for herself, be other than an innocent pastime, if they two—sure to be separated by their different paths in life, to-morrow—were to gather up some of the little pleasures that chanced to grow about their feet, like the violets and wood-anemones, to-day.

Yet an impulse of rectitude impelled Miriam to give him what she still held to be a needless warning against an imaginary peril.

"If you were wiser, Donatello, you would think me a dangerous person," said she. "If you follow my footsteps, they will lead you to no good. You ought to be afraid of me."

"I would as soon think of fearing the air we breathe," he replied.

"And well you may, for it is full of malaria," said Miriam; she went on, hinting at an intangible confession, such as persons with overburdened hearts often make to children or dumb animals, or to holes in the earth, where they think their secrets may be at once revealed and buried. "Those who come too near me are in danger of great mischiefs, I do assure you.

Take warning therefore! It is a sad fatality that has brought you from your home among the Apennines—some rusty old castle, I suppose, with a village at its foot, and an Arcadian environment of vineyards, fig-trees, and olive-orchards—a sad mischance, I say, that has transported you to my side. You have had a happy life hitherto—have you not, Donatello?"

"Oh, yes," answered the young man; and, though not of a retrospective turn, he made the best effort he could to send his mind back into the past. "I remember thinking it happiness to dance with the contadinas at a village feast; to taste the new sweet wine at vintage-time, and the old ripened wine, which our podere is famous for in the cold winter evenings; and to devour great, luscious figs, and apricots, peaches, cherries, and melons. I was often happy in the woods, too, with hounds and horses, and very happy in watching all sorts of creatures and birds that haunt the leafy solitudes. But never half so happy as now!"

"In these delightful groves?" she asked.

"Here, and with you," answered Donatello. "Just as we are now."

"What a fulness of content in him! How silly, and how delightful!" said Miriam to herself. Then addressing him again: "But, Donatello, how long will this happiness last?"

"How long!" he exclaimed; for it perplexed him even more to think of the future than to remember the past. "Why should it have any end? How long! For ever! for ever! for ever!"

"The child! the simpleton!" said Miriam, with sudden laughter, and checking it as suddenly. "But is he a simpleton indeed? Here, in those few natural words, he has expressed that deep sense, that profound conviction of its own immortality, which genuine love never fails to bring. He perplexes me—yes, and bewitches me—wild, gentle, beautiful creature that he is! It is like playing with a young greyhound!"

Her eyes filled with tears, at the same time that a smile shone out of them. Then first she became sensible of a delight and grief at once in feeling this zephyr of a new affection, with its untainted freshness, blow over her weary, stifled heart, which had no right to be revived by it. The very exquisiteness of the enjoyment made her know that it ought to be a forbidden one.

"Donatello," she hastily exclaimed, "for your own sake, leave me! It is not such a happy thing as you imagine it, to wander in these woods with me, a girl from another land, burdened with a doom that she tells to none. I might make you dread me—perhaps hate me—if I chose; and I must choose, if I find you loving me too well!"

"I fear nothing!" said Donatello, looking into her unfathomable eyes with perfect trust. "I love always!"

"I speak in vain," thought Miriam within herself. "Well, then, for this one hour, let me be such as he imagines me. To-morrow will be time enough to come back to my reality. My reality! what is it? Is the past so indestructible? the future so immitigable? Is the dark dream, in which I walk, of such solid, stony substance, that there can be no escape out of its dungeon? Be it so! There is, at least, that ethereal quality in my spirit, that it can make me as gay as Donatello himself—for this one hour!"

And immediately she brightened up, as if an inward flame, heretofore stifled, were now permitted to fill her with its happy lustre, glowing through her cheeks and dancing in her eyebeams.

Donatello, brisk and cheerful as he seemed before, showed a sensibility to Miriam's gladdened mood by breaking into still wilder and ever-varying activity. He frisked around her, bubbling over with joy, which clothed itself in words that had little individual meaning, and in snatches of song that seemed as natural as bird-notes. Then they both laughed together, and heard their own laughter returning in the echoes, and laughed again at the response; so that the ancient and solemn grove became full of merriment for these two blithe spirits. A bird happening to sing cheerily, Donatello gave a peculiar call, and the little feathered creature came fluttering about his head, as if it had known him through many summers.

"How close he stands to nature!" said Miriam, observing this pleasant familiarity between her companion and the bird. "Hes hall make me as natural as himself for this one hour."

As they strayed through that sweet wilderness, she felt more and more the influence of his elastic temperament. Miriam was an impressible and impulsive creature, as unlike herself, in different moods, as if a melancholy maiden and a glad one were both bound within the girdle about her waist, and kept in magic thraldom by the brooch that clasped it. Naturally, it is true, she was the more inclined to melancholy, yet fully capable of that high frolic of the spirits which richly compensates for many gloomy hours; if her soul was apt to lurk in the darkness of a cavern, she could sport madly in the sunshine before the cavern's mouth. Except the freshest mirth of animal spirits, like Donatello's, there is no merriment, no wild exhilaration, comparable to that of melancholy people escaping from the dark region in which it is their custom to keep themselves imprisoned.

So the shadowy Miriam almost outdid Donatello on his own ground. They ran races with each other, side by side, with shouts and laughter; they pelted one another with early flowers, and gathering them up again, twined them with green leaves into garlands for both their heads. They played together like children, or creatures of immortal youth. So much had they flung aside the sombre habitudes of daily life, that they seemed born to be sportive for ever, and endowed with eternal mirthfulness instead of any deeper joy. It was a glimpse far backward into Arcadian life, or, farther still, into the Golden Age, before mankind was burdened with sin and sorrow, and before pleasure had been darkened with those shadows that bring it into high relief, and make it happiness.

"Hark!" cried Donatello, stopping short, as he was about to bind Miriam's fair hands with flowers, and lead her along in triumph, "there is music somewhere in the grove!"

"It is your kinsman Pan, most likely," said Miriam, "playing on his pipe. Let us go seek him, and make him puff out his rough cheeks and pipe his merriest air! Come; the strain of music will guide us onward like a gaily coloured thread of silk."

"Or like a chain of flowers," responded Donatello, drawing her along by that which he had twined. "This way!—Come!"

CHAPTER X.

The Sylvan Dance.

As the music came fresher on their ears, they danced to its cadence, extemporizing new steps and attitudes. Each varying movement had a grace which might have been worth putting into marble, for the long delight of days to come, but vanished with the movement that gave it birth, and was effaced from memory by another. In Miriam's motion, freely as she flung herself into the frolic of the hour, there was still an artful beauty; in Donatello's, there was a charm of indescribable grotesqueness, hand in hand with grace; sweet, bewitching, most provocative of laughter, and yet akin to pathos, so deeply did it touch the heart. This was the ultimate peculiarity, the final touch, distinguishing between the sylvan creature and the beautiful companion at his side. Setting apart only this, Miriam resembled a Nymph, as much as Donatello did a Faun.

There were flitting moments, indeed, when she played the sylvan character as perfectly as he. Catching glimpses of her then, you would have fancied that an oak had sundered its rough bark to let her dance freely forth, endowed with the same spirit in her human form as that which rustles in the leaves; or that she had emerged through the pebbly bottom of a fountain, a water-nymph to play and sparkle in the sunshine, flinging a quivering light around her, and suddenly disappearing in a shower of rainbow drops.

As the fountain sometimes subsides into its basin, so in Miriam there were symptoms that the frolic of her spirits would at last tire itself out.

"Ah! Donatello," cried she, laughing, as she stopped to take breath; "you have an unfair advantage over me! I am no true creature of the woods; while you are a real Faun, I do believe. When your curls shook just now, methought I had a peep at the pointed ears."

Donatello snapped his fingers above his head, as fauns and satyrs taught us first to do, and seemed to radiate jollity out of his whole nimble person. Nevertheless, there was a kind of dim apprehension in his face, as if he dreaded that a moment's pause might break the spell, and snatch away the sportive companion whom he had waited for through so many dreary months.

"Dance! dance!" cried he, joyously. "If we take breath, we shall be as we were yesterday. There, now, is the music, just beyond this clump of trees. Dance, Miriam, dance!"

They had now reached an open, grassy glade (of which there are many in that artfully constructed wilderness), set round with stone seats, on which the aged moss had kindly essayed to spread itself instead of cushions. On one of the stone benches sat the musicians, whose strains had enticed our wild couple thitherward. They proved to be a vagrant band, such as Rome, and all Italy, abounds with; comprising a harp, a flute, and a violin, which, though greatly the worse for wear, the performers had skill enough to provoke and modulate into tolerable harmony. It chanced to be a feast-day; and, instead of playing in the sun-scorched piazzas of the city, or beneath the windows of some unresponsive palace, they had bethought themselves to try the echoes of these woods; for, on the festas of the Church, Rome scatters its merry-makers all abroad, ripe for the dance or any other pastime.

As Miriam and Donatello emerged from among the trees the musicians scraped, tinkled, or blew, each according to his various kind of instrument, more inspiringly than ever. A dark-cheeked little girl, with bright black eyes, stood by, shaking a tambourine set round with tinkling bells, and thumping it on its parchment head. Without interrupting his brisk, though measured movement, Donatello snatched away this unmelodious contrivance, and flourishing it above his head, produced music of indescribable potency, still dancing with frisky step, and striking the tambourine, and ringing its little bells, all in one jovial act.

It might be that there was magic in the sound, or contagion, at least, in the spirit which had got possession of Miriam and himself, for very soon a number of festal people were drawn to the spot, and struck into the dance, singly, or in pairs, as if they were all gone mad with jollity. Among them were some of the plebeian damsels whom we meet bare-headed in the Roman streets, with silver stilettos thrust through their glossy hair; the contadinas, too, from the Campagna and the villages, with their rich and picturesque costumes of scarlet and all bright hues, such as fairer maidens might not venture to put on. Then came the modern Roman from Trastevere, perchance, with his old cloak drawn about him like a toga, which anon, as his active motion heated him, he flung aside. Three French soldiers capered freely into the throng, in wide scarlet trousers, their short swords dangling at their sides; and three German artists in gray flaccid hats and flaunting beards; and one of the Pope's Swiss guardsmen in the strange motley garb which Michael Angelo contrived for them. Two young English tourists (one of them a lord) took contadine partners and dashed in, as did also a shaggy man in goat-skin breeches, who looked like rustic Pan in person, and footed it as merrily as he. Besides the above there was a herdsman or two from the Campagna, and a few peasants in sky-blue jackets, and small-clothes tied with ribbons at the knees; haggard and sallow were these last, poor serfs, having little to eat and nothing but the malaria to breathe; but still they plucked up a momentary spirit and joined hands in Donatello's dance.

Here, as it seemed, had the Golden Age come back again within the precincts of this sunny glade, thawing mankind out of their cold formalities, releasing them from irksome restraint, mingling them together in such childlike gaiety that new flowers (of which the old bosom of the earth is full) sprang up beneath their footsteps. The sole exception to the geniality of the moment, as we have understood, was seen in a countryman of our own, who sneered at the spectacle, and declined to compromise his dignity by making part of it.

The harper thrummed with rapid fingers; the violin-player flashed his bow back and forth across the strings; the flautist poured his breath in quick puffs of jollity, while Donatello shook the tambourine above his head, and led the merry throng with unweariable steps. As they followed one another in a wild ring of mirth, it seemed the realization of one of those bas-reliefs where a dance of nymphs, satyrs, or bacchanals is twined around the circle of an antique vase; or it was like the sculptured scene on the front and sides of a sarcophagus, where, as often as any other device, a festive procession mocks the ashes and white bones that are treasured up within. You might take it for a marriage-pageant; but after a while, if you look at these merry-makers, following them from end to end of the marble coffin, you doubt whether their gay movement is leading them to a happy close. A youth has suddenly fallen in the dance; a chariot is overturned and broken, flinging the charioteer headlong to the ground; a maiden seems to have grown faint or weary and is drooping on the bosom of a friend. Always some tragic incident is shadowed forth or thrust sidelong into the spectacle; and when once it has caught your eye you can look no more at the festal portions of the scene except with reference to this one slightly suggested doom and sorrow.

As in its mirth, so in the darker characteristic here alluded to, there was an analogy between the sculptured scene on the sarcophagus and the wild dance which we have been describing. In the midst of its madness and riot Miriam found herself suddenly confronted by a strange figure that shook its fantastic garments in the air, and pranced before her on its tiptoes, almost vying with the agility of Donatello himself. It was the model.

A moment afterwards Donatello was aware that she had retired from the dance. He hastened towards her, and flung himself on the grass beside the stone bench on which Miriam was sitting. But a strange distance and unapproachableness had all at once enveloped her; and though he saw her within reach of his arm, yet the light of her eyes seemed as far off as that of a star, nor was there any warmth in the melancholy smile with which she regarded him.

"Come back!" cried he. "Why should this happy hour end so soon?"

"It must end here, Donatello," said she, in answer to his words and outstretched hand; "and such hours, I believe, do not often repeat themselves in a lifetime. Let me go, my friend; let me vanish from you quietly among the shadows of these trees. See, the companions of our pastime are vanishing already!"

Whether it was that the harp-strings were broken,

the violin out of tune, or the flautist out of breath, so it chanced that the music had ceased, and the dancers come abruptly to a pause. All that motley throng of rioters was dissolved as suddenly as it had been drawn together. In Miriam's remembrance the scene had a character of fantasy. It was as if a company of satyrs, fauns, and nymphs, with Pan in the midst of them, had been disporting themselves in these venerable woods only a moment ago; and now in another moment, because some profane eye had looked at them too closely, or some intruder had cast a shadow on their mirth, the silver pageant had utterly disappeared. If a few of the merry-makers lingered among the trees, they had hidden their racy peculiarities under the garb and aspect of ordinary people, and sheltered themselves in the weary commonplace of daily life. Just an instant before it was Arcadia and the Golden Age. The spell being broken, it was now only that old tract of pleasure-ground, close by the people's gate of Rome,—a tract where the crimes and calamities of ages, the many battles, blood recklessly poured out, and deaths of myriads, have corrupted all the soil, creating an influence that makes the air deadly to human lungs.

"You must leave me," said Miriam to Donatello, more imperatively than before: "have I not said it? Go; and look not behind you."

"Miriam," whispered Donatello, grasping her hand forcibly, "who is it that stands in the shadow yonder, beckoning you to follow him?"

"Hush; leave me!" repeated Miriam. "Your hour is past; his hour has come."

Donatello still gazed in the direction which he had indicated, and the expression of his face was fearfully changed, being so disordered, perhaps with terror—at all events with anger and invincible repugnance—that Miriam hardly knew him. His lips were drawn apart so as to disclose his set teeth, thus giving him a look of animal rage, which we seldom see except in persons of the simplest and rudest natures. A shudder seemed to pass through his very bones.

"I hate him!" muttered he.

"Be satisfied; I hate him too!" said Miriam.

She had no thought of making this avowal, but was irresistibly drawn to it by the sympathy of the dark emotion in her own breast with that so strongly expressed by Donatello. Two drops of water or of blood do not more naturally flow into each other than did her hatred into his.

"Shall I clutch him by the throat?" whispered Donatello, with a savage scowl. "Bid me do so, and we are rid of him for ever."

"In Heaven's name, no violence!" exclaimed Miriam, affrighted out of the scornful control which she had hitherto held over her companion, by the fierceness that he so suddenly developed. "Oh, have pity on me, Donatello, if for nothing else, yet because in the midst of my wretchedness I let myself be your playmate for this one wild hour. Follow me no farther. Henceforth, leave me to my doom. Dear friend—kind, simple, loving friend—make me not more wretched by the remembrance of having thrown fierce hates or loves into the wellspring of your happy life!"

"Not follow you!" repeated Donatello, soothed from anger into sorrow, less by the purport of what she said, than by the melancholy sweetness of her voice. "Not follow you! What other path have I?"

"We will talk of it once again," said Miriam, still soothingly; "soon—to-morrow—when you will; only leave me now."

CHAPTER XI.

Fragmentary Sentences.

In the Borghese Grove, so recently uproarious with merriment and music, there remained only Miriam and her strange follower.

A solitude had suddenly spread itself around them. It perhaps symbolized a peculiar character in the relation of these two, insulating them, and building up an insuperable barrier between their life-streams and other currents, which might seem to flow in close vicinity. For it is one of the chief earthly incommodities of some species of misfortune, or of a great crime, that it makes the actor in the one, or the sufferer of the other, an alien in the world, by interposing a wholly unsympathetic medium betwixt himself and those whom he yearns to meet.

Owing, it may be, to this moral estrangement—this chill remoteness of their position—there have come to us but a few vague whisperings of what passed in Miriam's interview that afternoon with the sinister personage who had dogged her footsteps ever since the visit to the catacomb. In weaving these mystic utterances into a continuous scene, we undertake a task resembling in its perplexity that of gathering up and piecing together the fragments of a letter which has been torn and scattered to the winds. Many words of deep significance, many entire sentences, and those possibly the most important ones, have flown too far on the winged breeze to be recovered. If we insert our own conjectural amendments, we perhaps give a purport utterly at variance with the true one. Yet unless we attempt something in this way, there must remain an unsightly gap, and a lack of continuousness and dependence in our narrative; so that it would arrive at certain inevitable catastrophes without due warning of their imminence.

Of so much we are sure, that there seemed to be a sadly mysterious fascination in the influence of this ill-omened person over Miriam; it was such as beasts and reptiles of subtle and evil nature sometimes exercise upon their victims. Marvellous it was to see the hopelessness with which—being naturally of so courageous a spirit—she resigned herself to the thraldom in which he held her. That iron chain, of which some of the massive links were round her feminine waist, and the others in his ruthless hand—or which, perhaps, bound the pair together by a bond equally torturing to each—must have been forged in some such unhallowed furnace as is only kindled by evil passions and fed by evil deeds.

Yet, let us trust, there may have been no crime in Miriam, but only one of those fatalities which are among the most insoluble riddles propounded to mortal comprehension; the fatal decree by which every crime is made to be the agony of many innocent persons, as well as of the single guilty one.

It was, at any rate, but a feeble and despairing kind of remonstrance which she had now the energy to oppose against his persecution.

"You follow me too closely," she said, in low, faltering accents; "you allow me too scanty room to draw my breath. Do you know what will be the end of this?"

"I know well what must be the end," he replied.

"Tell me, then," said Miriam, "that I may compare your foreboding with my own. Mine is a very dark one."

"There can be but one result, and that soon," answered the model. "You must throw off your present mask and assume another. You must vanish out of the scene: quit Rome with me, and leave no trace whereby to follow you. It is in my power, as you well know, to compel your acquiescence in my bidding. You are aware of the penalty of a refusal."

"Not that penalty with which you would terrify me," said Miriam; "another there may be, but not so grievous."

"What is that other?" he inquired.

"Death! simply, death!" she answered.

"Death," said her persecutor, "is not so simple and opportune a thing as you imagine. You are strong and warm with life. Sensitive and irritable as your spirit is, these many months of trouble, this latter thraldom in which I hold you, have scarcely made your cheek paler than I saw it in your girlhood. Miriam,—for I forbear to speak another name, at which these leaves would shiver above our heads,—Miriam, you cannot die!"

"Might not a dagger find my heart?" said she, for the first time meeting his eyes. "Would not poison make an end of me? Will not the Tiber drown me?"

"It might," he answered; "for I allow that you are mortal. But, Miriam, believe me, it is not your fate to die while there remains so much to be sinned and suffered in the world. We have a destiny which we must needs fulfil together. I, too, have struggled to escape it. I was as anxious as yourself to break the tie between us—to bury the past in a fathomless grave—to make it impossible that we should ever meet, until you confront me at the bar of Judgment! You little can imagine what steps I took to render all this secure; and what was the result? Our strange interview in the bowels of the earth convinced me of the futility of my design."

"Ah, fatal chance!" cried Miriam, covering her face with her hands.

"Yes, your heart trembled with horror when you recognized me," rejoined he; "but you did not guess that there was an equal horror in my own!"

"Why would not the weight of earth above our heads have crumbled down upon us both forcing us apart, but burying us equally?" cried Miriam, in a burst of vehement passion. "Oh, that we could have wandered in those dismal passages till we both perished, taking opposite paths in the darkness, so that when we lay down to die our last breaths might not mingle!"

"It were vain to wish it," said the model. "In all that labyrinth of midnight paths, we should have found one another out to live or die together. Our fates cross and are entangled. The threads are twisted into a strong cord, which is dragging us to an evil doom. Could the knots be severed, we might escape. But neither can your slender fingers untie those knots, nor my masculine force break them. We must submit!"

"Pray for rescue, as I have," exclaimed Miriam. "Pray for deliverance from me, since I am your evil genius, as you mine. Dark as your life has been, I have known you to pray in times past!"

At these words of Miriam, a tremor and horror appeared to seize upon her persecutor, insomuch that he shook and grew ashy pale before her eyes. In this man's memory, there was something that made it awful for him to think of prayer; nor would any torture be more intolerable, than to be reminded of such divine comfort and succour as await pious souls merely for the asking. This torment was perhaps the token of a native temperament deeply susceptible of religious impressions, but which had been wronged, violated, and debased, until, at length, it was capable only of terror from the sources that were intended for our purest and loftiest consolation. He looked so fearfully at her, and with such intense pain struggling in his eyes, that Miriam felt pity.

And, now, all at once, it struck her that he might be mad. It was an idea that had never before seriously occurred to her mind, although, as soon as suggested, it fitted marvellously into many circumstances that lay within her knowledge. But, alas! such was her evil fortune, that, whether mad or no, his power over her remained the same, and was likely to be used only the more tyrannously if exercised by a lunatic.

"I would not give you pain," she said, soothingly; "your faith allows you the consolations of penance and absolution. Try what help there may be in these, and leave me to myself."

"Do not think it, Miriam," said he; "we are bound together, and can never part again."

"Why should it seem so impossible?" she rejoined. "Think how I had escaped from all the past! I had made for myself a new sphere, and found new friends, new occupations, new hopes and enjoyments. My heart, methinks, was almost as unburthened as if there had been no miserable life behind me. The human spirit does not perish of a single wound, nor exhaust itself in a single trial of life. Let us but keep asunder, and all may go well for both."

"We fancied ourselves for ever sundered," he replied. "Yet we met once, in the bowels of the earth; and, were we to part now, our fates would fling us together again in a desert, on a mountain-top, or in whatever spot seemed safest. You speak in vain, therefore."

"You mistake your own will for an iron necessity," said Miriam; "otherwise, you might have suffered me to glide past you like a ghost, when we met among those ghosts of ancient days. Even now you might bid me pass as freely."

"Never!" said he, with unmitigable will; "your reappearance has destroyed the work of years. You know the power that I have over you. Obey my bidding; or, within short time it shall be exercised: nor will I cease to haunt you till the moment comes."

"Then," said Miriam, more calmly, "I foresee the end, and have already warned you of it. It will be death!"

"Your own death, Miriam—or mine?" he asked, looking fixedly at her.

"Do you imagine me a murderess?" said she, shuddering; "you, at least, have no right to think me so!"

"Yet," rejoined he, with a glance of dark meaning, "men have said that this white hand had once a crimson stain." He took her hand as he spoke, and held it in his own, in spite of the repugnance, amounting to nothing short of agony, with which she struggled to regain it. Holding it up to the fading light (for there was already dimness among the trees), he appeared to examine it closely, as if to discover the imaginary blood-stain with which he taunted her. He smiled as he let it go. "It looks very white," said he; "but I have known hands as white, which all the water in the ocean would not have washed clean."

"It had no stain," retorted Miriam, bitterly, "until you grasped it in your own."

The wind has blown away whatever else they may have spoken.

They went together towards the town, and, on their way, continued to make reference, no doubt, to some strange and dreadful history of their former life, belonging equally to this dark man and to the fair and youthful woman, whom he persecuted. In their words, or in the breath that uttered them, there seemed to be an odour of guilt, and a scent of blood. Yet, how can we imagine that a stain of ensanguined crime should attach to Miriam! Or, how, on the other hand, should spotless innocence be subjected to a thraldom like that which she endured from the spectre, whom she herself had evoked out of the darkness! Be this as it might, Miriam, we have reason to believe, still continued to beseech him, humbly, passionately, wildly, only to go his way, and leave her free to follow her own sad path.

Thus they strayed onward through the green wilderness of the Borghese grounds, and soon came near the city wall, where, had Miriam raised her eyes, she might have seen Hilda and the sculptor leaning on the parapet. But she walked in a mist of trouble, and could distinguish little beyond its limits. As they came within public observation, her persecutor fell behind, throwing off the imperious manner which he had assumed during their solitary interview. The Porta del Popolo swarmed with life. The merry-makers, who had spent the feast-day outside the walls, were now thronging in; a party of horsemen were entering beneath the arch; a travelling-carriage had been drawn up just within the verge, and was passing through the villanous ordeal of the papal custom-house. In the broad piazza, too, there was a motley crowd.

But the stream of Miriam's trouble kept its way through this flood of human life, and neither mingled with it nor was turned aside. With a sad kind of feminine ingenuity, she found a way to kneel before her tyrant, undetected, though in full sight of all the people, still beseeching him for freedom, and in vain.

CHAPTER XII.

A Stroll on the Pincian.

HILDA, after giving the last touches to the picture of Beatrice Cenci, had flown down from her dovecote, late in the afternoon, and gone to the Pincian Hill, in the hope of hearing a strain or two of exhilarating music. There, as it happened, she met the sculptor; for, to say the truth, Kenyon had well noted the fair artist's ordinary way of life, and was accustomed to shape his own movements so as to bring him often within her sphere.

The Pincian Hill is the favourite promenade of the Roman aristocracy. At the present day, however, like most other Roman possessions, it belongs less to the native inhabitants than to the barbarians from Gaul, Great Britain, and beyond the sea, who have established a peaceful usurpation over whatever is enjoyable or memorable in the Eternal City. These foreign guests are indeed ungrateful, if they do not breathe a prayer for Pope Clement, or whatever Holy Father it may have been, who levelled the summit of the mount so skilfully, and bounded it with the parapet of the city wall; who laid out those broad walks and drives, and overhung them with the deepening shade of many kinds of tree; who scattered the flowers of all seasons, and of every clime, abundantly over those green, central lawns; who scooped out hollows in fit places, and setting great basins of marble in them, caused ever-gushing fountains to fill them to the brim; who reared up the immemorial obelisk out of the soil that had long hidden it; who placed pedestals along the borders of the avenues, and crowned them with busts of that multitude of worthies—statesmen, heroes, artists, men of letters, and of song—whom the whole world claims as its chief ornaments though Italy produced them all. In a word, the Pincian garden is one of the things that reconcile the stranger (since he fully appreciates the enjoyment, and feels nothing of the cost) to the rule of an irresponsible dynasty of Holy Fathers, who seem to have aimed at making life as agreeable an affair as it can well be.

In this pleasant spot the red-trowsered French soldiers are always to be seen; bearded and grizzled veterans, perhaps, with medals of Algiers or the Crimea on their breasts. To them is assigned the peaceful duty of seeing that children do not trample on the flower-beds, nor any youthful lover rifle them of their fragrant blossoms to stick in the beloved one's hair. Here sits (drooping upon some marble bench, in the treacherous sunshine) the consumptive girl, whose friends have brought her, for cure, to a climate that instils poison into its very purest breath. Here, all day, come nursery-maids, burdened with rosy English babies, or guiding the footsteps of little travellers from the far Western world. Here, in the sunny afternoons, roll and rumble all kinds of equipages, from the cardinal's old-fashioned and gorgeous purple carriage to the gay barouche of modern date. Here horsemen gallop on thorough-bred steeds. Here, in short, all the transitory population of Rome, the world's great watering-place, rides, drives, or promenades! Here are beautiful sunsets; and here, whichever way you turn your eyes, are scenes as well worth gazing at, both in themselves and for their historic interest, as any that the sun ever rose and set upon. Here, too, on certain afternoons of the week, a French military band flings out rich music over the poor old city, floating her with strains as loud as those of her own echoless triumphs.

Hilda and the sculptor (by the contrivance of the latter, who loved best to be alone with his young countrywoman) had wandered beyond the throng of promenaders, whom they left in a dense cluster around the music. They strayed, indeed, to the farthest point of the Pincian Hill, and leaned over the parapet, looking down upon the Muro Torto, a massive fragment of the oldest Roman wall, which juts over, as if ready to tumble down by its own weight, yet seems still the most indestructible piece of work that men's hands ever piled together. In the blue distance, rose Soracte, and other heights, which have gleamed afar, to our imaginations, but look scarcely real to our bodily eyes, because, being dreamed about so much, they have taken the aërial tints which belong only to a dream. These, nevertheless, are the solid framework of hills that shut in Rome, and its wide surrounding Campagna; no land of dreams, but the broadest page of history, crowded so full with memorable events that one obliterates another; as if Time had crossed and recrossed his own records till they grew illegible.

But, not to meddle with history—with which our narrative is not otherwise concerned, than that the very dust of Rome is historic, and inevitably settles on our page and mingles with our ink—we will return to our two friends, who were still leaning over the wall. Beneath them lay the broad sweep of the Borghese grounds, covered with trees, amid which appeared the white gleam of pillars and statues, and the flash of an upspringing fountain, all to be overshadowed at a later period of the year, by the thicker growth of foliage.

The advance of vegetation, in this softer climate, is less abrupt than the inhabitant of the cold North is accustomed to observe. Beginning earlier—even in February—Spring is not compelled to burst into Summer with such headlong haste; there is time to dwell upon each opening beauty, and to enjoy the budding leaf, the tender green, the sweet youth and freshness of the year; it gives us its maiden charm, before settling into the married Summer, which, again, does not so soon sober itself into matronly Autumn. In our own country, the virgin Spring hastens to its bridal too abruptly. But, here, after a month or two of kindly growth, the leaves of the young trees, which cover that portion of the Borghese grounds nearest the city wall, were still in their tender half-development.

In the remoter depths, among the old groves of ilex-trees, Hilda and Kenyon heard the faint sound of music, laughter, and mingling voices. It was probably the uproar—spreading even so far as the walls of Rome, and growing faded and melancholy in its passage—of that wild sylvan merriment, which we have already attempted to describe. By and by, it ceased; although the two listeners still tried to distinguish it between the bursts of nearer music from the military band. But there was no renewal of that distant mirth. Soon afterwards, they saw a solitary figure, advancing along one of the paths that lead from the obscurer part of the grounds, towards the gateway.

"Look! is it not Donatello?" said Hilda.

"He it is, beyond a doubt," replied the sculptor. "But how gravely he walks, and with what long looks behind him! He seems either very weary, or very sad. I should not hesitate to call it sadness, if Donatello were a creature capable of the sin and folly of low spirits. In all these hundred paces, while we have been watching him, he has not made one of those little caprioles in the air, which are a characteristic of his natural gait. I begin to doubt whether he is a veritable Faun."

"Then," said Hilda, with perfect simplicity, "you have thought him—and do think him—one of that strange, wild, happy race of creatures, that used to laugh and sport in the woods, in the old, old times? So do I, indeed! But I never quite believed, till now, that fauns existed anywhere but in poetry."

The sculptor at first merely smiled. Then, as the idea took further possession of his mind, he laughed outright, and wished from the bottom of his heart (being in love with Hilda, though he had never told her so) that he could have rewarded or punished her for its pretty absurdity with a kiss.

"Oh, Hilda, what a treasure of sweet faith and pure imagination you hide under that little straw hat!" cried he, at length. "A Faun! a Faun! Great Pan is not dead, then, after all! The whole tribe of mythical creatures yet live in the moonlit seclusion of a young girl's fancy, and find it a lovelier abode and play-place, I doubt not, than their Arcadian haunts of yore. What bliss, if a man of marble, like myself, could stray thither too!"

"Why do you laugh so?" asked Hilda, reddening; for she was a little disturbed at Kenyon's ridicule, however kindly expressed. "What can I have said, that you think so very foolish?"

"Well, not foolish, then," rejoined the sculptor, "but wiser, it may be, than I can fathom. Really, however, the idea does strike one as delightfully fresh, when we consider Donatello's position and external environment. Why, my dear Hilda, he is a Tuscan born, of an old noble race in that part of Italy; and he has a moss-grown tower among the Apennines, where he and his forefathers have dwelt, under their own vines and fig-trees, from an unknown antiquity. His boyish passion for Miriam has introduced him familiarly to our little circle; and our republican and artistic simplicity of intercourse has included this young Italian, on the same terms as one of ourselves. But, if we paid due respect to rank and title, we should bend reverentially to Donatello, and salute him as his Excellency the Count di Monte Beni."

"That is a droll idea — much droller than his being a Faun!" said Hilda, laughing in her turn. "This does not quite satisfy me, however, especially as you yourself recognized and acknowledged his wonderful resemblance to the statue."

"Except as regards the pointed ears," said Kenyon; adding, aside—"and one other little peculiarity, generally observable in the statues of fauns."

"As for his Excellency the Count di Monte Beni's ears," replied Hilda, smiling again at the dignity with which this title invested their playful friend, "you know we could never see their shape, on account of his clustering curls. Nay, I remember, he once started back, as shyly as a wild deer, when Miriam made a pretence of examining them. How do you explain that?"

"Oh, I certainly shall not contend against such a weight of evidence; the fact of his faunship being otherwise so probable," answered the sculptor, still hardly retaining his gravity. "Faun or not, Donatello —or the Count di Monte Beni—is a singularly wild creature, and, as I have remarked on other occasions, though very gentle, does not love to be touched. Speaking in no harsh sense, there is a great deal of animal nature in him, as if he had been born in the woods, and had run wild all his childhood, and were as yet but imperfectly domesticated. Life, even in our day, is very simple and unsophisticated in some of the shaggy nooks of the Apennines."

"It annoys me very much," said Hilda, "this inclination, which most people have, to explain away the wonder and the mystery out of everything. Why could not you allow me—and yourself, too—the satisfaction of thinking him a Faun?"

"Pray keep your belief, dear Hilda, if it makes you any happier," said the sculptor; "and I shall do my best to become a convert. Donatello has asked me to spend the summer with him, in his ancestral tower, where I purpose investigating the pedigree of these sylvan counts, his forefathers; and if their shadows beckon me into dreamland, I shall willingly follow. By the by, speaking of Donatello, there is a point on which I should like to be enlightened."

"Can I help you, then?" said Hilda, in answer to his look.

"Is there the slightest chance of his winning Miriam's affections?" suggested Kenyon.

"Miriam! she, so accomplished and gifted!" exclaimed Hilda—"and he, a rude, uncultivated boy! No, no, no!"

"It would seem impossible," said the sculptor. "But, on the other hand, a gifted woman flings away her affections so unaccountably, sometimes! Miriam, of late, has been very morbid and miserable, as we both know. Young as she is, the morning light seems already to have faded out of her life; and now comes

Donatello, with natural sunshine enough for himself and her, and offers her the opportunity of making her heart and life all new and cheery again. People of high intellectual endowments do not require similar ones in those they love. They are just the persons to appreciate the wholesome gush of natural feeling, the honest affection, the simple joy, the fulness of contentment with what he loves, which Miriam sees in Donatello. True; she may call him a simpleton. It is a necessity of the case; for a man loses the capacity for this kind of affection, in proportion as he cultivates and refines himself."

"Dear me!" said Hilda, drawing imperceptibly away from her companion. "Is this the penalty of refinement? Pardon me; I do not believe it. It is because you are a sculptor, that you think nothing can be finely wrought, except it be cold and hard, like the marble in which your ideas take shape. I am a painter, and know that the most delicate beauty may be softened and warmed throughout."

"I said a foolish thing, indeed," answered the sculptor. "It surprises me, for I might have drawn a wiser knowledge out of my own experience. It is the surest test of genuine love, that it brings back our early simplicity to the worldliest of us."

Thus talking, they loitered slowly along beside the parapet which borders the level summit of the Pincian with its irregular sweep. At intervals they looked through the lattice-work of their thoughts at the varied prospects that lay before and beneath them.

From the terrace where they now stood there is an abrupt descent towards the Piazza del Popolo; and looking down into its broad space they beheld the tall, palatial edifices, the church-domes, and the ornamented gateway, which grew and were consolidated out of the thought of Michael Angelo. They saw, too, the red granite obelisk, oldest of things, even in Rome, which rises in the centre of the piazza, with a fourfold fountain at its base. All Roman works and ruins (whether of the empire, the far-off republic, or the still more distant kings) assume a transient, visionary, and impalpable character when we think that this indestructible monument supplied one of the recollections which Moses and the Israelites bore from Egypt into the desert. Perchance, on beholding the cloudy pillar and the fiery column, they whispered awe-stricken to one another, "In its shape it is like that old obelisk which we and our fathers have so often seen on the borders of the Nile." And now that very obelisk, with hardly a trace of decay upon it, is the first thing that the modern traveller sees after entering the Flaminian Gate!

Lifting their eyes, Hilda and her companion gazed westward, and saw beyond the invisible Tiber the Castle of St. Angelo; that immense tomb of a pagan emperor, with the archangel at its summit.

Still farther off appeared a mighty pile of buildings, surmounted by the vast dome, which all of us have shaped and swelled outward, like a huge bubble, to the utmost scope of our imaginations, long before we see it floating over the worship of the city. It may be most worthily seen from precisely the point where our two friends were now standing. At any nearer view the grandeur of St. Peter's hides itself behind the immensity of its separate parts, so that we see only the front, only the sides, only the pillared length and loftiness of the portico, and not the mighty whole. But at this distance the entire outline of the world's cathedral, as well as that of the palace of the world's chief priest, is taken in at once. In such remoteness, moreover, the imagination is not debarred from lending its assistance, even while we have the reality before our eyes, and helping the weakness of human sense to do justice to so grand an object. It requires both faith and fancy to enable us to feel, what is nevertheless so true, that yonder, in front of the purple outline of hills, is the grandest edifice ever built by man, painted against God's loveliest sky.

After contemplating a little while a scene which their long residence in Rome had made familiar to them, Kenyon and Hilda again let their glances fall into the piazza at their feet. They there beheld Miriam, who had just entered the Porta del Popolo, and was standing by the obelisk and fountain. With a gesture that impressed Kenyon as at once suppliant and imperious, she seemed to intimate to a figure which had attended her thus far, that it was now her desire to be left alone. The pertinacious model, however, remained immoveable.

And the sculptor here noted a circumstance, which,

according to the interpretation he might put upon it, was either too trivial to be mentioned, or else so mysteriously significant that he found it difficult to believe his eyes. Miriam knelt down on the steps of the fountain; so far there could be no question of the fact. To other observers, if any there were, she probably appeared to take this attitude merely for the convenience of dipping her fingers into the gush of water from the mouth of one of the stone lions. But as she clasped her hands together after thus bathing them, and glanced upward at the model, an idea took strong possession of Kenyon's mind that Miriam was kneeling to this dark follower there in the world's face!

"Do you see it?" he said to Hilda.

"See what?" asked she, surprised at the emotion of his tone. "I see Miriam, who has just bathed her hands in that delightfully cool water. I often dip my fingers into a Roman fountain, and think of the brook that used to be one of my playmates in my New England village."

"I fancied I saw something else," said Kenyon; "but it was doubtless a mistake."

But, allowing that he had caught a true glimpse into the hidden significance of Miriam's gesture, what a terrible thraldom did it suggest! Free as she seemed to be—beggar as he looked—the nameless vagrant must then be dragging the beautiful Miriam through the streets of Rome, fettered and shackled more cruelly than any captive queen of yore following in an emperor's triumph. And was it conceivable that she would have been thus enthralled unless some great error—how great Kenyon dared not think—or some fatal weakness had given this dark adversary a vantage-ground?

"Hilda," said he, abruptly, "who and what is Miriam? Pardon me; but are you sure of her?"

"Sure of her!" repeated Hilda, with an angry blush, for her friend's sake. "I am sure that she is kind, good, and generous; a true and faithful friend, whom I love dearly, and who loves me as well! What more than this need I be sure of?"

"And your delicate instincts say all this in her favour?—nothing against her?" continued the sculptor, without heeding the irritation of Hilda's tone. "These are my own impressions, too. But she is such a mystery! We do not even know whether she is a countrywoman of ours, or an Englishwoman, or a German. There is Anglo-Saxon blood in her veins, one would say, and a right English accent on her tongue, but much that is not English breeding, nor American. Nowhere else but in Rome, and as an artist, could she hold a place in society without giving some clue to her past life."

"I love her dearly," said Hilda, still with displeasure in her tone, "and trust her most entirely."

"My heart trusts her at least, whatever my head may do," replied Kenyon; "and Rome is not like one of our New England villages, where we need the permission of each individual neighbour for every act that we do, every word that we utter, and every friend that we make or keep. In these particulars the papal despotism allows us freer breath than our native air; and if we like to take generous views of our associates, we can do so, to a reasonable extent, without ruining ourselves."

"The music has ceased," said Hilda; "I am going now."

There are three streets that, beginning close beside each other, diverge from the Piazza del Popolo towards the heart of Rome: on the left, the Via del Babuino; on the right, the Via della Ripetta; and between these two that world-famous avenue, the Corso. It appeared that Miriam and her strange companion were passing up the first-mentioned of these three, and were soon hidden from Hilda and the sculptor.

The two latter left the Pincian by the broad and stately walk that skirts along its brow. Beneath them, from the base of the abrupt descent, the city spread wide away in a close contiguity of red-earthen roofs, above which rose eminent the domes of a hundred churches, besides here and there a tower, and the upper windows of some taller or higher situated palace, looking down on a multitude of palatial abodes. At a distance, ascending out of the central mass of edifices, they could see the top of the Antonine column, and near it the circular roof of the Pantheon, looking heavenward with its ever-open eye.

Except these two objects, almost everything that they beheld was mediæval, though built, indeed, of the massive old stones and indestructible bricks of imperial

Rome; for the ruin of the Coliseum, the Golden House, and innumerable temples of Roman gods, and mansions of Cæsars and senators, had supplied the material for all those gigantic hovels, and their walls were cemented with mortar of inestimable cost, being made of precious antique statues, burnt long ago for this petty purpose.

Rome, as it now exists, has grown up under the Popes, and seems like nothing but a heap of broken rubbish, thrown into the great chasm between our own days and the Empire, merely to fill it up; and, for the better part of two thousand years, its annals of obscure policies, and wars, and continually recurring misfortunes, seem also but broken rubbish, as compared with its classic history.

If we consider the present city as at all connected with the famous one of old, it is only because we find it built over its grave. A depth of thirty feet of soil has covered up the Rome of ancient days, so that it lies like the dead corpse of a giant, decaying for centuries, with no survivor mighty enough even to bury it, until the dust of all those years has gathered slowly over its recumbent form and made a casual sepulchre.

We know not how to characterize, in any accordant and compatible terms, the Rome that lies before us; its sunless alleys, and streets of palaces; its churches, lined with the gorgeous marbles that were originally polished for the adornment of pagan temples; its thousands of evil smells, mixed up with fragrance of rich incense, diffused from as many censers; its little life, deriving feeble nutriment from what has long been dead. Everywhere, some fragment of ruin suggesting the magnificence of a former epoch; everywhere, moreover, a Cross—and nastiness at the foot of it. As the sum of all, there are recollections that kindle the soul, and a gloom and languor that depress it beyond any depth of melancholic sentiment that can be elsewhere known.

Yet how is it possible to say an unkind or irreverential word of Rome? The city of all time, and of all the world! The spot for which man's great life and deeds have done so much, and for which decay has done whatever glory and dominion could not do! At this moment, the evening sunshine is flinging its golden mantle over it, making all that we thought mean magnificent; the bells of all the churches suddenly ring out, as if it were a peal of triumph because Rome is still imperial.

"I sometimes fancy," said Hilda, on whose susceptibility the scene always made a strong impression, "that Rome—mere Rome—will crowd everything else out of my heart."

"Heaven forbid!" ejaculated the sculptor.

They had now reached the grand stairs that ascend from the Piazza di Spagna to the hither brow of the Pincian Hill. Old Beppo, the millionnaire of his ragged fraternity—it is a wonder that no artist paints him as the cripple whom St. Peter heals at the Beautiful Gate of the Temple—was just mounting his donkey to depart, laden with the rich spoil of the day's beggary.

Up the stairs, drawing his tattered cloak about his face, came the model, at whom Beppo looked askance, jealous of an encroacher on his rightful domain. The figure passed away, however, up the Via Sistina. In the piazza below, near the foot of the magnificent steps, stood Miriam, with her eyes bent on the ground, as if she were counting those little, square, uncomfortable paving stones, that make it a penitential pilgrimage to walk in Rome. She kept this attitude for several minutes, and when, at last, the importunities of a beggar disturbed her from it, she seemed bewildered, and pressed her hand upon her brow.

"She has been in some sad dream or other, poor thing!" said Kenyon, sympathizingly; "and even now, she is imprisoned there in a kind of cage, the iron bars of which are made of her own thoughts."

"I fear she is not well," said Hilda. "I am going down the stairs, and will join Miriam."

"Farewell, then," said the sculptor. "Dear Hilda, this is a perplexed and troubled world! It soothes me inexpressibly to think of you in your tower, with white doves and white thoughts for your companions, so high above us all, and with the Virgin for your household friend. You know not how far it throws its light, that lamp, which you keep burning at her shrine! I passed beneath the tower last night, and the ray cheered me —because you lighted it."

"It has for me a religious significance," replied Hilda, quietly, "and yet I am no Catholic."

They parted, and Kenyon made haste along the Via Sistina, in the hope of overtaking the model, whose haunts and character he was anxious to investigate, for Miriam's sake. He fancied that he saw him a long way in advance, but before he reached the Fountain of the Triton, the dusky figure had vanished.

CHAPTER XIII.

A Sculptor's Studio.

About this period, Miriam seems to have been goaded by a weary restlessness, that drove her abroad on any errand or none. She went one morning to visit Kenyon in his studio, whither he had invited her to see a new statue, on which he had staked many hopes, and which was now almost completed in the clay. Next to Hilda, the person for whom Miriam felt most affection and confidence was Kenyon; and in all the difficulties that beset her life, it was her impulse to draw near Hilda for feminine sympathy, and the sculptor for brotherly counsel.

Yet it was to little purpose that she approached the edge of the voiceless gulf between herself and them. Standing on the utmost verge of that dark chasm, she might stretch out her hand, and never clasp a hand of theirs; she might strive to call out, "Help, friends! help!" but, as with dreamers when they shout, her voice would perish inaudibly in the remoteness that seemed such a little way. This perception of an infinite, shivering solitude, amid which we cannot come close enough to human beings to be warmed by them, and where they turn to cold, chilly shapes of mist, is one of the most forlorn results of any accident, misfortune, crime, or peculiarity of character, that puts an individual ajar with the world. Very often, as in Miriam's case, there is an insatiable instinct that demands friendship, love, and intimate communion, but is forced to pine in empty forms; a hunger of the heart, which finds only shadows to feed upon.

Kenyon's studio was in a cross-street, or, rather, an ugly and dirty little lane, between the Corso and the Via della Ripetta; and though chill, narrow, gloomy, and bordered with tall and shabby structures, the lane was not a whit more disagreeable than nine-tenths of the Roman streets. Over the door of one of the houses was a marble tablet, bearing an inscription, to the purport that the sculpture-rooms within had formerly been occupied by the illustrious artist Canova. In these precincts (which Canova's genius was not quite of a character to render sacred, though it certainly made them interesting) the young American sculptor had now established himself.

The studio of a sculptor is generally but a rough and dreary-looking place, with a good deal the aspect, indeed, of a stone-mason's workshop. Bare floors of brick or plank, and plastered walls; an old chair or two, or perhaps only a block of marble (containing, however, the possibility of ideal grace within it), to sit down upon; some hastily scrawled sketches of nude figures on the whitewash of the wall. These last are probably the sculptor's earliest glimpses of ideas that may hereafter be solidified into imperishable stone, or perhaps may remain as impalpable as a dream. Next there are a few very roughly modelled little figures in clay or plaster, exhibiting the second stage of the idea as it advances towards a marble immortality; and then is seen the exquisitely designed shape of clay, more interesting than even the final marble, as being the intimate production of the sculptor himself, moulded throughout with his loving hands, and nearest to his imagination and heart. In the plaster-cast, from this clay model, the beauty of the statue strangely disappears, to shine forth again with pure, white radiance, in the precious marble of Carrara. Works in all these stages of advancement, and some with the final touch upon them, might be found in Kenyon's studio.

Here might be witnessed the process of actually chiselling the marble, with which (as it is not quite satisfactory to think) a sculptor, in these days, has very little to do. In Italy, there is a class of men whose merely mechanical skill is perhaps more exquisite than was possessed by the ancient artificers, who wrought out the designs of Praxiteles; or, very possibly, by Praxiteles himself. Whatever of illusive representation can be effected in marble, they are capable of achieving, if the object be before their eyes. The sculptor has but to present these men with a plaster-cast of his design, and a sufficient block of marble, and tell them that the figure is imbedded in the stone, and must be freed from its encumbering superfluities; and, in due time, without the necessity of his touching the work with his own finger, he will see before him the statue that is to make him renowned. His creative power has wrought it with a word.

In no other art, surely, does genius find such effective instruments, and so happily relieve itself of the drudgery of actual performance; doing wonderfully nice things by the hands of other people, when it may be suspected they could not always be done by the sculptor's own. And how much of the admiration which our artists get for their buttons and button-holes, their shoe-ties, their neck-cloths,—and these, at our present epoch of taste, make a large share of the renown,—would be abated, if we were generally aware that the sculptor can claim no credit for such pretty performances, as immortalized in marble! They are not his work, but that of some nameless machine in human shape.

Miriam stopped an instant in an antechamber, to look at a half-finished bust, the features of which seemed to be struggling out of the stone; and, as it were, scattering and dissolving its hard substance by the glow of feeling and intelligence. As the skilful workman gave stroke after stroke of the chisel with apparent carelessness, but sure effect, it was impossible not to think that the outer marble was merely an extraneous environment; the human countenance within its embrace must have existed there since the limestone ledges of Carrara were first made. Another bust was nearly completed, though still one of Kenyon's most trustworthy assistants was at work, giving delicate touches, shaving off an impalpable something, and leaving little heaps of marble-dust to attest it.

"As these busts in the block of marble," thought Miriam, "so does our individual fate exist in the limestone of time. We fancy that we carve it out; but its ultimate shape is prior to all our action."

Kenyon was in the inner room, but, hearing a step in the antechamber, he threw a veil over what he was at work upon, and came out to receive his visitor. He was dressed in a gray blouse, with a little cap on the top of his head; a costume which became him better than the formal garments which he wore, whenever he passed out of his own domains. The sculptor had a face which, when time had done a little more for it, would offer a worthy subject for as good an artist as himself; features finely cut, as if already marble; an ideal forehead, deeply set eyes, and a mouth much hidden in a light-brown beard, but apparently sensitive and delicate.

"I will not offer you my hand," said he; "it is grimy with Cleopatra's clay."

"No; I will not touch clay; it is earthy and human," answered Miriam. "I have come to try whether there is any calm and coolness among your marbles. My own art is too nervous, too passionate, too full of agitation, for me to work at it whole days together, without intervals of repose. So, what have you to show me?"

"Pray look at everything here," said Kenyon. "I love to have painters see my work. Their judgment

is unprejudiced, and more valuable than that of the world generally, from the light which their own art throws on mine. More valuable, too, than that of my brother sculptors, who never judge me fairly—nor I them, perhaps."

To gratify him, Miriam looked round at the specimens in marble or plaster, of which there were several in the room, comprising originals or casts of most of the designs that Kenyon had thus far produced. He was still too young to have accumulated a large gallery of such things. What he had to show were chiefly the attempts and experiments, in various directions, of a beginner in art, acting as a stern tutor to himself, and profiting more by his failures than by any successes of which he was yet capable. Some of them, however, had great merit; and, in the pure, fine glow of the new marble, it may be, they dazzled the judgment into awarding them higher praise than they deserved. Miriam admired the statue of a beautiful youth, a pearl-fisher, who had got entangled in the weeds at the bottom of the sea, and lay dead among the pearl-oysters, the rich shells, and the sea-weeds, all of like value to him now.

"The poor young man has perished among the prizes that he sought," remarked she. "But what a strange efficacy there is in death! If we cannot all win pearls, it causes an empty shell to satisfy us just as well. I like this statue, though it is too cold and stern in its moral lesson; and, physically, the form has not settled itself into sufficient repose."

In another style, there was a grand, calm head of Milton, not copied from any one bust or picture, yet more authentic than any of them, because all known representations of the poet had been profoundly studied, and solved in the artist's mind. The bust over the tomb in Grey Friars Church, the original miniatures and pictures, wherever to be found, had mingled each its special truth in this one work; wherein, likewise, by long perusal and deep love of the *Paradise Lost*, the *Comus*, the *Lycidas*, and *L'Allegro*, the sculptor had succeeded, even better than he knew, in spiritualizing his marble with the poet's mighty genius. And this was a great thing to have achieved, such a length of time after the dry bones and dust of Milton were like those of any other dead man.

There were also several portrait-busts, comprising those of two or three of the illustrious men of our own country, whom Kenyon, before he left America, had asked permission to model. He had done so, because he sincerely believed that, whether he wrought the busts in marble or bronze, the one would corrode and the other crumble, in the long lapse of time, beneath these great men's immortality. Possibly, however, the young artist may have under-estimated the durability of his material. Other faces there were, too, of men who (if the brevity of their remembrance, after death, can be argued from their little value in life) should have been represented in snow rather than marble. Posterity will be puzzled what to do with busts like these, the concretions and petrifactions of a vain self-estimate; but will find, no doubt, that they serve to build into stone walls, or burn into quicklime, as well as if the marble had never been blocked into the guise of human heads.

But it is an awful thing, indeed, this endless endurance, this almost indestructibility, of a marble bust! Whether in our own case, or that of other men, it bids us sadly measure the little, little time, during which our lineaments are likely to be of interest to any human being. It is especially singular that Americans should care about perpetuating themselves in this mode. The brief duration of our families, as a hereditary household, renders it next to a certainty that the great-grandchildren will not know their father's grandfather, and that half a century hence, at farthest, the hammer of the auctioneer will thump its knock-down blow against his blockhead, sold at so much for the pound of stone! And it ought to make us shiver, the idea of leaving our features to be a dusty-white ghost among strangers of another generation, who will take our nose between their thumb and fingers (as we have seen men do by Cæsar's), and infallibly break it off, if they can do so without detection!

"Yes," said Miriam, who had been revolving some such thoughts as the above, "it is a good state of mind for mortal man, when he is content to leave no more definite memorial than the grass, which will sprout kindly and speedily over his grave, if we do not make the spot barren with marble. Methinks, too, it will be a fresher and better world, when it flings off this great burthen of stony memories, which the ages have deemed it a piety to heap upon its back."

"What you say," remarked Kenyon, "goes against my whole art. Sculpture, and the delight which men naturally take in it, appear to me a proof that it is good to work with all time before our view."

"Well, well," answered Miriam, "I must not quarrel with you for flinging your heavy stones at poor Posterity; and, to say the truth, I think you are as likely to hit the mark as anybody. These busts, now, much as I seem to scorn them, make me feel as if you were a magician. You turn feverish men into cool, quiet marble. What a blessed change for them! Would you could do as much for me!"

"Oh, gladly!" cried Kenyon, who had long wished to model that beautiful and most expressive face. "When will you begin to sit?"

"Poh! that was not what I meant," said Miriam. "Come, show me something else."

"Do you recognize this?" asked the sculptor.

He took out of his desk a little old-fashioned ivory coffer, yellow with age; it was richly carved with antique figures and foliage; and had Kenyon thought fit to say that Benvenuto Cellini wrought this precious box, the skill and elaborate fancy of the work would by no means have discredited his word, nor the old artist's fame. At least, it was evidently a production of Benvenuto's school and century, and might once have been the jewel-case of some grand lady at the court of the De' Medici.

Lifting the lid, however, no blaze of diamonds was disclosed, but only, lapt in fleecy cotton, a small, beautifully shaped hand, most delicately sculptured in marble. Such loving care and nicest art had been lavished here, that the palm really seemed to have a tenderness in its very substance. Touching those lovely fingers—had the jealous sculptor allowed you to touch—you could hardly believe that a virgin warmth would not steal from them into your heart.

"Ah, this is very beautiful!" exclaimed Miriam, with a genial smile. "It is as good in its way as Loulie's hand with its baby-dimples, which Powers showed me at Florence, evidently valuing it as much as if he had wrought it out of a piece of his great heart. As good as Harriet Hosmer's clasped hands of Browning and his wife, symbolizing the individuality and heroic union of two high, poetic lives! Nay, I do not question that it is better than either of those, because you must have wrought it passionately, in spite of its maiden palm and dainty finger-tips."

"Then you do recognize it?" asked Kenyon.

"There is but one right hand on earth that could have supplied the model," answered Miriam; "so small and slender, so perfectly symmetrical, and yet with a character of delicate energy. I have watched it a hundred times at its work; but I did not dream that you had won Hilda so far! How have you persuaded that shy maiden to let you take her hand in marble?"

"Never! She never knew it!" hastily replied Kenyon, anxious to vindicate his mistress's maidenly reserve.

"I stole it from her. The hand is a reminiscence. After gazing at it so often, and even holding it once for an instant when Hilda was not thinking of me, I should be a bungler indeed if I could not now reproduce it to something like the life."

"May you win the original one day!" said Miriam, kindly.

"I have little ground to hope it," answered the sculptor, despondingly; "Hilda does not dwell in our mortal atmosphere; and gentle and soft as she appears, it will be as difficult to win her heart as to entice down a white bird from its sunny freedom in the sky. It is strange, with all her delicacy and fragility, the impression she makes of being utterly sufficient to herself. No; I shall never win her. She is abundantly capable of sympathy, and delights to receive it, but she has no need of love."

"I partly agree with you," said Miriam. "It is a mistaken idea, which men generally entertain, that nature has made women especially prone to throw their whole being into what is technically called love. We have, to say the least, no more necessity for it than yourselves; only we have nothing else to do with our hearts. When women have other objects in life, they are not apt to fall in love. I can think of many women distinguished in art, literature, and science—and multitudes whose hearts and minds find good employment in less ostentatious ways—who lead high, lonely lives, and are conscious of no sacrifice so far as your sex is concerned."

"And Hilda will be one of these!" said Kenyon, sadly; "the thought makes me shiver for myself, and —and for her, too."

"Well," said Miriam, smiling, "perhaps she may sprain the delicate wrist which you have sculptured to such perfection. In that case you may hope. These old masters to whom she has vowed herself, and whom her slender hand and woman's heart serve so faithfully, are your only rivals."

The sculptor sighed as he put away the treasure of Hilda's marble hand into the ivory coffer, and thought how slight was the possibility that he should ever feel responsive to his own the tender clasp of the original. He dared not even kiss the image that he himself had made; it had assumed its share of Hilda's remote and shy divinity.

"And now," said Miriam, "show me the new statue which you asked me hither to see."

CHAPTER XIV.

Cleopatra.

"My new statue!" said Kenyon, who had positively forgotten it in the thought of Hilda; "here it is under this veil."

"Not a nude figure, I hope," observed Miriam. "Every young sculptor seems to think that he must give the world some specimen of indecorous womanhood, and call it Eve, Venus, a Nymph, or any name that may apologize for a lack of decent clothing. I am weary, even more than I am ashamed, of seeing such things. Now-a-days people are as good as born in their clothes, and there is practically not a nude human being in existence. An artist, therefore, as you must candidly confess, cannot sculpture nudity with a pure heart, if only because he is compelled to steal guilty glimpses at hired models. The marble inevitably loses its chastity under such circumstances. An old Greek sculptor, no doubt, found his models in the open sunshine, and among pure and princely maidens, and thus the nude statues of antiquity are as modest as violets, and sufficiently draped in their own beauty. But as for Mr. Gibson's coloured Venuses (stained, I believe, with tobacco-juice), and all other nudities of to-day, I really do not understand what they have to say to this generation, and would be glad to see as many heaps of quicklime in their stead."

"You are severe upon the professors of my art," said Kenyon, half smiling, half seriously; "not that you are wholly wrong, either. We are bound to accept drapery of some kind, and make the best of it. But what are we to do? Must we adopt the costume of to-day, and carve, for example, a Venus in a hoop-petticoat?"

"That would be a boulder, indeed!" rejoined Miriam, laughing. "But the difficulty goes to confirm me in my belief that, except for portrait-busts, sculpture has no longer a right to claim any place among living arts. It has wrought itself out, and come fairly to an end. There is never a new group now-a-days; never even so much as a new attitude. Greenough (I take my examples among men of merit) imagined nothing new; nor Crawford either, except in the tailoring line. There are not, as you will own, more than half a dozen positively original statues or groups in the world, and these few are of immemorial antiquity. A person familiar with the Vatican, the Uffizzi Gallery, the Naples Gallery, and the Louvre, will at once refer any modern production to its antique prototype; which, moreover, had begun to get out of fashion, even in old Roman days."

"Pray stop, Miriam," cried Kenyon, "or I shall fling away the chisel for ever!"

"Fairly own to me, then, my friend," rejoined Miriam, whose disturbed mind found a certain relief in this declamation, "that you sculptors are, of necessity, the greatest plagiarists in the world."

"I do not own it," said Kenyon, "yet cannot utterly contradict you, as regards the actual state of the art. But as long as the Carrara quarries still yield pure blocks, and while my own country has marble mountains, probably as fine in quality, I shall steadfastly believe that future sculptors will revive this noblest of the beautiful arts, and people the world with new shapes of delicate grace and massive grandeur. Perhaps," he added, smiling, "mankind will consent to wear a more manageable costume; or, at worst, we sculptors shall get the skill to make broadcloth transparent, and render a majestic human character visible through the coats and trousers of the present day."

"Be it so!" said Miriam; "you are past my counsel. Show me the veiled figure, which, I am afraid, I have criticized beforehand. To make amends, I am in the mood to praise it now."

But, as Kenyon was about to take the cloth off the clay model, she laid her hand on his arm.

"Tell me first what is the subject," said she, "for I have sometimes incurred great displeasure from members of your brotherhood by being too obtuse to puzzle out the purport of their productions. It is so difficult, you know, to compress and define a character or story, and make it patent at a glance, within the narrow scope attainable by sculpture! Indeed, I fancy it is still the ordinary habit with sculptors, first to finish their group of statuary—in such development as the particular block of marble will allow—and then to choose the subject; as John of Bologna did with his 'Rape of the Sabines.' Have you followed that good example?"

"No; my statue is intended for Cleopatra," replied Kenyon, a little disturbed by Miriam's raillery. "The special epoch of her history you must make out for yourself."

He drew away the cloth that had served to keep the moisture of the clay model from being exhaled. The sitting figure of a woman was seen. She was draped from head to foot in a costume minutely and scrupulously studied from that of ancient Egypt, as revealed by the strange sculpture of that country, its coins, drawings, painted mummy-cases, and whatever other tokens have been dug out of its pyramids, graves, and catacombs. Even the stiff Egyptian head-dress was adhered to, but had been softened into a rich feminine adornment, without losing a particle of its truth. Difficulties that might well have seemed insurmountable, had been courageously encountered and made flexible to purposes of grace and dignity; so that Cleopatra sat attired in a garb proper to her historic and queenly state, as a daughter of the Ptolemies, and yet such as the beautiful woman would have put on as best adapted to heighten the magnificence of her charms, and kindle a tropic fire in the cold eyes of Octavius.

A marvellous repose—that rare merit in statuary, except it be the lumpish repose native to the block of stone—was diffused throughout the figure. The spectator felt that Cleopatra had sunk down out of the fever and turmoil of her life, and for one instant—as it were, between two pulse-throbs—had relinquished all activity, and was resting throughout every vein and muscle. It was the repose of despair, indeed; for Octavius had seen her, and remained insensible to her enchantments. But still there was a great smouldering furnace deep down in the woman's heart. The repose, no doubt, was as complete as if she were never to stir hand or foot again; and yet, such was the creature's latent energy and fierceness, she might spring upon you like a tigress, and stop the very breath that you were now drawing midway in your throat.

The face was a miraculous success. The sculptor had not shunned to give the full, Nubian lips, and other characteristics of the Egyptian physiognomy. His courage and integrity had been abundantly rewarded; for Cleopatra's beauty shone out richer, warmer, more triumphantly beyond comparison, than if, shrinking timidly from the truth, he had chosen the tame Grecian type. The expression was of profound, gloomy, heavily revolving thought; a glance into her past life and present emergencies, while her spirit gathered itself up for some new struggle, or was getting sternly reconciled to impending doom. In one view, there was a certain softness and tenderness—how breathed into the statue, among so many strong and passionate elements, it is impossible to say. Catching another glimpse, you beheld her as implacable as a stone and cruel as fire.

In a word, all Cleopatra—fierce, voluptuous, passionate, tender, wicked, terrible, and full of poisonous and rapturous enchantment—was kneaded into what, only a week or two before, had been a lump of wet clay from the Tiber. Soon, apotheosized in an indestructible material, she would be one of the images that men keep for ever, finding a heat in them which does not cool down, throughout the centuries.

"What a woman is this!" exclaimed Miriam, after a long pause. "Tell me, did she ever try, even while you were creating her, to overcome you with her fury or her love? Were you not afraid to touch her, as she grew more and more towards hot life beneath your hand? My dear friend, it is a great work! How have you learned to do it?"

"It is the concretion of a good deal of thought, emotion, and toil of brain and hand," said Kenyon, not without a perception that his work was good; "but I know not how it came about at last. I kindled a great fire within my mind, and threw in the material—as Aaron threw the gold of the Israelites into the furnace—and in the midmost heat uprose Cleopatra, as you see her."

"What I most marvel at," said Miriam, "is the womanhood that you have so thoroughly mixed up with all those seemingly discordant elements. Where did you get that secret? You never found it in your gentle Hilda: yet I recognize its truth."

"No, surely, it was not in Hilda," said Kenyon.

"Her womanhood is of the ethereal type, and incompatible with any shadow of darkness or evil."

"You are right," rejoined Miriam; "there are women of that ethereal type as you term it, and Hilda is one of them. She would die of her first wrong-doing—supposing for a moment that she could be capable of doing wrong. Of sorrow, slender as she seems, Hilda might bear a great burden; of sin, not a feather's weight. Methinks now, were it my doom, I could bear either, or both at once; but my conscience is still as white as Hilda's. Do you question it?"

"Heaven forbid, Miriam!" exclaimed the sculptor.

He was startled at the strange turn which she had so suddenly given to the conversation. Her voice, too—so much emotion was stifled rather than expressed in it—sounded unnatural.

"Oh, my friend," cried she, with sudden passion, "will you be my friend indeed? I am lonely, lonely, lonely! There is a secret in my heart that burns me—that tortures me! Sometimes I fear to go mad of it; sometimes I hope to die of it, but neither of the two happens. Ah, if I could but whisper it to only one human soul! And you—you see far into womanhood; you receive it widely into your large view! Perhaps—perhaps, but Heaven only knows, you might understand me! Oh, let me speak!"

"Miriam, dear friend," replied the sculptor, "if I can help you, speak freely, as to a brother."

"Help me? No!" said Miriam.

Kenyon's response had been perfectly frank and

kind; and yet the subtlety of Miriam's emotion detected a certain reserve and alarm in his warmly expressed readiness to hear her story. In his secret soul, to say the truth, the sculptor doubted whether it were well for this poor suffering girl to speak what she so yearned to say, or for him to listen. If there were any active duty of friendship to be performed, then, indeed, he would joyfully have come forward to do his best. But if it were only a pent-up heart that sought an outlet? in that case it was by no means so certain that a confession would do good. The more her secret struggled and fought to be told, the more certain would it be to change all former relations that had subsisted between herself and the friend to whom she might reveal it. Unless he could give her all the sympathy, and just the kind of sympathy that the occasion required, Miriam would hate him by and by, and herself still more, if he let her speak.

This was what Kenyon said to himself; but his reluctance, after all, and whether he were conscious of it or no, resulted from a suspicion that had crept into his heart and lay there in a dark corner. Obscure as it was, when Miriam looked into his eyes, she detected it at once.

"Ah, I shall hate you!" cried she, echoing the thought which he had not spoken; she was half choked with the gush of passion that was thus turned back upon her. "You are as cold and pitiless as your own marble."

"No; but full of sympathy, God knows!" replied he.

In truth his suspicions, however warranted by the mystery in which Miriam was enveloped, had vanished in the earnestness of his kindly and sorrowful emotion. He was now ready to receive her trust.

"Keep your sympathy, then, for sorrows that admit of such solace," said she, making a strong effort to compose herself. "As for my griefs, I know how to manage them. It was all a mistake: you can do nothing for me, unless you petrify me into a marble companion for your Cleopatra there; and I am not of her sisterhood, I do assure you. Forget this foolish scene, my friend, and never let me see a reference to it in your eyes when they meet mine hereafter."

"Since you desire it, all shall be forgotten," answered the sculptor, pressing her hand as she departed; "or, if ever I can serve you, let my readiness to do so be remembered. Meanwhile, dear Miriam, let us meet in the same clear, friendly light as heretofore."

"You are less sincere than I thought you," said Miriam, "if you try to make me think that there will be no change."

As he attended her through the antechamber, she pointed to the statue of the pearl-diver.

"My secret is not a pearl," said she; "yet a man might drown himself in plunging after it."

After Kenyon had closed the door, she went wearily down the staircase, but paused midway, as if debating with herself whether to return.

"The mischief was done," thought she; "and I might as well have had the solace that ought to come with it. I have lost—by staggering a little way beyond the mark, in the blindness of my distress—I have lost, as we shall hereafter find, the genuine friendship of this clear-minded, honourable, true-hearted young man, and all for nothing. What if I should go back this moment and compel him to listen?"

She ascended two or three of the stairs, but again paused, murmured to herself, and shook her head.

"No, no, no," she thought; "and I wonder how I ever came to dream of it. Unless I had his heart for my own—and that is Hilda's, nor would I steal it from her—it should never be the treasure-place of my secret. It is no precious pearl, as I just now told him; but my dark-red carbuncle—red as blood—is too rich a gem to put into a stranger's casket."

She went down the stairs and found her Shadow waiting for her in the street.

CHAPTER XV.

An Æsthetic Company.

On the evening after Miriam's visit to Kenyon's studio, there was an assemblage, composed almost entirely of Anglo-Saxons, and chiefly of American artists, with a sprinkling of their English brethren; and some few of the tourists who still lingered in Rome, now that Holy Week was past. Miriam, Hilda, and the sculptor, were all three present, and, with them, Donatello, whose life was so far turned from its natural bent, that, like a pet spaniel, he followed his beloved mistress wherever he could gain admittance.

The place of meeting was in the palatial, but somewhat faded and gloomy apartment of an eminent member of the æsthetic body. It was no more formal an occasion than one of those weekly receptions, common among the foreign residents of Rome, at which pleasant people—or disagreeable ones, as the case may be—encounter one another with little ceremony.

If anywise interested in art, a man must be difficult to please who cannot find fit companionship among a crowd of persons, whose ideas and pursuits all tend towards the general purpose of enlarging the world's stock of beautiful productions.

One of the chief causes that make Rome the favourite residence of artists—their ideal home which they sigh for in advance, and are so loth to migrate from, after once breathing its enchanted air—is, doubtless, that they there find themselves in force, and are numerous enough to create a congenial atmosphere. In every other clime they are isolated strangers; in this land of art, they are free citizens.

Not that, individually, or in the mass, there appears to be any large stock of mutual affection among the brethren of the chisel and the pencil. On the contrary, it will impress the shrewd observer that the jealousies and petty animosities, which the poets of our day have flung aside, still irritate and gnaw into the hearts of this kindred class of imaginative men. It is not difficult to suggest reasons why this should be the fact. The public, in whose good graces lie the sculptor's or the painter's prospects of success, is infinitely smaller than the public to which literary men make their appeal. It is composed of a very limited body of wealthy patrons; and these, as the artist well knows, are but blind judges in matters that require the utmost delicacy of perception. Thus, success in art is apt to become partly an affair of intrigue; and it is almost inevitable that even a gifted artist should look askance at his gifted brother's fame, and be chary of the good word that might help him to sell still another statue or picture. You seldom hear a painter heap generous praise on anything in his special line of art; a sculptor never has a favourable eye for any marble but his own.

Nevertheless, in spite of all these professional

grudges, artists are conscious of a social warmth from each other's presence and contiguity. They shiver at the remembrance of their lonely studios in the unsympathizing cities of their native land. For the sake of such brotherhood as they can find, more than for any good that they get from galleries, they linger year after year in Italy, while their originality dies out of them, or is polished away as a barbarism.

The company this evening included several men and women whom the world has heard of, and many others, beyond all question, whom it ought to know. It would be a pleasure to introduce them upon our humble pages, name by name, and—had we confidence enough in our own taste—to crown each well-deserving brow according to its deserts. The opportunity is tempting, but not easily manageable, and far too perilous, both in respect to those individuals whom we might bring forward, and the far greater number that must needs be left in the shade. Ink, moreover, is apt to have a corrosive quality, and might chance to raise a blister, instead of any more agreeable titillation, on skins so sensitive as those of artists. We must therefore forego the delight of illuminating this chapter with personal allusions to men whose renown glows richly on canvas, or gleams in the white moonlight of marble.

Otherwise we might point to an artist who has studied nature with such tender love that she takes him to her intimacy, enabling him to reproduce her in landscapes that seem the reality of a better earth, and yet are but the truth of the very scenes around us, observed by the painter's insight and interpreted for us by his skill. By his magic, the moon throws her light far out of the picture, and the crimson of the summer night absolutely glimmers on the beholder's face. Or we might indicate a poet-painter, whose song has the vividness of picture, and whose canvas is peopled with angels, fairies, and water-sprites, done to the ethereal life, because he saw them face to face in his poetic mood. Or we might bow before an artist, who has wrought too sincerely, too religiously, with too earnest a feeling, and too delicate a touch, for the world at once to recognize how much toil and thought are compressed into the stately brow of Prospero, and Miranda's maiden loveliness; or from what a depth within this painter's heart the Angel is leading forth St. Peter.

Thus it would be easy to go on, perpetrating a score of little epigrammatical allusions, like the above, all kindly meant, but none of them quite hitting the mark, and often striking where they were not aimed. It may be allowable to say, however, that American art is much better represented at Rome in the pictorial than in the sculpturesque department. Yet the men of marble appear to have more weight with the public than the men of canvas; perhaps on account of the greater density and solid substance of the material in which they work, and the sort of physical advantage which their labours thus acquire over the illusive unreality of colour. To be a sculptor, seems a distinction in itself; whereas, a painter is nothing, unless individually eminent.

One sculptor there was, an Englishman, endowed with a beautiful fancy, and possessing at his fingers' ends the capability of doing beautiful things. He was a quiet, simple, elderly personage, with eyes brown and bright, under a slightly impending brow, and a Grecian profile, such as he might have cut with his own chisel. He had spent his life, for forty years, in making Venuses, Cupids, Bacchuses, and a vast deal of other marble progeny of dream-work, or rather frost-work: it was all a vapoury exhalation out of the Grecian mythology, crystallizing on the dull window-panes of to-day. Gifted with a more delicate power than any other man alive, he had foregone to be a Christian reality, and perverted himself into a Pagan idealist, whose business or efficacy, in our present world, it would be exceedingly difficult to define. And, loving and reverencing the pure material in which he wrought, as surely this admirable sculptor did, he had nevertheless robbed the marble of its chastity, by giving it an artificial warmth of hue. Thus it became a sin and shame to look at his nude goddesses. They had revealed themselves to his imagination, no doubt, with all their deity about them; but, bedaubed with buff-colour, they stood forth to the eyes of the profane in the guise of naked women. But, whatever criticism may be ventured on his style, it was good to meet a man so modest, and yet imbued with such thorough and simple conviction of his own right principles and practice, and so quietly satisfied that his kind of antique achievement was all that sculpture could effect for modern life.

This eminent person's weight and authority among his artistic brethren were very evident; for beginning unobtrusively to utter himself on a topic of art, he was soon the centre of a little crowd of younger sculptors. They drank in his wisdom, as if it would serve all the purposes of original inspiration; he, meanwhile, discoursing with gentle calmness, as if there could possibly be no other side, and often ratifying, as it were, his own conclusions by a mildly emphatic—"Yes."

The veteran sculptor's unsought audience was composed mostly of our own countrymen. It is fair to say, that they were a body of very dexterous and capable artists, each of whom had probably given the delighted public a nude statue, or had won credit for even higher skill by the nice carving of button-holes, shoe-ties, coat-seams, shirt-bosoms, and other such graceful peculiarities of modern costume. Smart, practical men they doubtless were, and some of them far more than this, but, still, not precisely what an uninitiated person looks for in a sculptor. A sculptor, indeed, to meet the demands which our preconceptions make upon him, should be even more indispensably a poet than those who deal in measured verse and rhyme. His material, or instrument, which serves him in the stead of shifting and transitory language, is a pure, white, undecaying substance. It ensures immortalily to whatever is wrought in it, and therefore makes it a religious obligation to commit no idea to its mighty guardianship, save such as may repay the marble for its faithful care, its incorruptible fidelity, by warming it with an ethereal life. Under this aspect, marble assumes a sacred character: and no man should dare to touch it unless he feels within himself a certain consecration and a priesthood, the only evidence of which, for the public eye, will be the high treatment of heroic subjects, or the delicate evolution of spiritual, through material beauty.

No ideas such as the foregoing—no misgivings suggested by them—probably troubled the self-complacency of most of these clever sculptors. Marble, in their view, had no such sanctity as we impute to it. It was merely a sort of white limestone from Carrara, cut into convenient blocks, and worth, in that state, about two or three dollars per pound; and it was susceptible of being wrought into certain shapes (by their own mechanical ingenuity, or that of artisans in their employment) which would enable them to sell it again at a much higher figure. Such men, on the strength of some small knack in handling clay, which might have been fitly employed in making waxwork, are bold to call themselves sculptors. How terrible should be the thought, that the nude woman whom the modern artist patches together, bit by bit, from a dozen heterogeneous models, meaning nothing by her, shall last as long as the Venus of the Capitol!—that his group of —no matter what, since it has no moral or intellectual existence—will not physically crumble any sooner than the immortal agony of the Laocoon!

Yet we love the artists, in every kind; even these, whose merits we are not quite able to appreciate. Sculptors, painters, crayon sketchers, or whatever branch of æsthetics they adopted, were certainly pleasanter people, as we saw them that evening, than the average whom we meet in ordinary society. They were not wholly confined within the sordid compass of practical life; they had a pursuit which, if followed faithfully out, would lead them to the beautiful, and always had a tendency thitherward, even if they lingered to gather up golden dross by the wayside. Their actual business (though they talked about it very much as other men talk of cotton, politics, flour-barrels, and sugar) necessarily illuminated their conversation with something akin to the ideal. So, when the guests collected themselves in little groups, here and there, in the wide saloon, a cheerful and airy gossip began to be heard. The atmosphere ceased to be precisely that of common life; a faint, mellow tinge, such as we see in pictures, mingled itself with the lamplight.

This good effect was assisted by many curious little treasures of art, which the host had taken care to strew upon his tables. They were principally such bits of antiquity as the soil of Rome and its neighbourhood are still rich in; seals, gems, small figures of bronze, mediæval carvings in ivory; things which had been obtained at little cost, yet might have borne no inconsiderable value in the museum of a virtuoso.

As interesting as any of these relics was a large portfolio of old drawings, some of which, in the opinion of their possessor, bore evidence on their faces of the touch of master-hands. Very ragged and ill-conditioned they mostly were, yellow with time, and tattered with rough usage; and, in their best estate, the designs had been scratched rudely with pen and ink, on coarse paper, or, if drawn with charcoal or a pencil, were now half rubbed out. You would not anywhere see rougher and homelier things than these. But this hasty rudeness made the sketches only the more valuable; because the artist seemed to have bestirred himself at the pinch of the moment, snatching up whatever material was nearest, so as to seize the first glimpse of an idea that might vanish in the twinkling of an eye. Thus, by the spell of a creased, soiled, and discoloured scrap of paper, you were enabled to steal close to an old master, and watch him in the very effervescence of his genius.

According to the judgment of several connoisseurs, Raphael's own hand had communicated its magnetism to one of these sketches; and, if genuine, it was evidently his first conception of a favourite Madonna, now hanging in the private apartment of the Grand Duke, at Florence. Another drawing was attributed to Leonardo da Vinci, and appeared to be a somewhat varied design for his picture of Modesty and Vanity, in the Sciarra Palace. There were at least half-a-dozen others, to which the owner assigned as high an origin. It was delightful to believe in their authenticity, at all events; for these things make the spectator more vividly sensible of a great painter's power, than the final glow and perfected art of the most consummate picture that may have been elaborated from them. There is an effluence of divinity in the first sketch; and there, if anywhere, you find the pure light of inspiration, which the subsequent toil of the artist serves to bring out in stronger lustre, indeed, but likewise adulterates it with what belongs to an inferior mood. The aroma and fragrance of new thought were perceptible in these designs, after three centuries of wear and tear. The charm lay partly in their very imperfection; for this is suggestive, and sets the imagination at work; whereas, the finished picture, if a good one, leaves the spectator nothing to do, and, if bad, confuses, stupefies, disenchants, and disheartens him.

Hilda was greatly interested in this rich portfolio. She lingered so long over one particular sketch, that Miriam asked her what discovery she had made.

"Look at it carefully," replied Hilda, putting the sketch into her hands. "If you take pains to disentangle the design from those pencil-marks, that seem to have been scrawled over it, I think you will see something very curious."

"It is a hopeless affair, I am afraid," said Miriam. "I have neither your faith, dear Hilda, nor your perceptive faculty. Fie! what a blurred scrawl it is indeed!"

The drawing had originally been very slight, and had suffered more from time and hard usage than almost any other in the collection; it appeared, too, that there had been an attempt (perhaps by the very hand that drew it) to obliterate the design. By Hilda's help, however, Miriam pretty distinctly made out a winged figure with a drawn sword, and a dragon, or a demon, prostrate at his feet.

"I am convinced," said Hilda, in a low, reverential tone, "that Guido's own touches are on that ancient scrap of paper! If so, it must be his original sketch for the picture of the Archangel Michael, setting his foot upon the demon, in the church of the Cappuccini. The composition and general arrangement of the sketch are the same with those of the picture; the only difference being, that the demon has a more upturned face, and scowls vindictively at the Archangel, who turns away his eyes in painful disgust."

"No wonder!" responded Miriam. "The expression suits the daintiness of Michael's character, as Guido represents him. He never could have looked the demon in the face!"

"Miriam!" exclaimed her friend, reproachfully, "you grieve me, and you know it, by pretending to speak contemptuously of the most beautiful and the divinest figure that mortal painter ever drew."

"Forgive me, Hilda!" said Miriam. "You take these matters more religiously than I can, for my life. Guido's Archangel is a fine picture, of course, but it never impressed me as it does you."

"Well; we will not talk of that," answered Hilda. "What I wanted you to notice, in this sketch, is the face of the demon. It is entirely unlike the demon of the finished picture. Guido, you know, always affirmed that the resemblance to Cardinal Pamfili was either casual or imaginary. Now, here is the face as he first conceived it."

"And a more energetic demon, altogether, than that of the finished picture," said Kenyon, taking the sketch into his hand. "What a spirit is conveyed into the ugliness of this strong, writhing, squirming dragon, under the Archangel's foot! Neither is the face an impossible one. Upon my word, I have seen it somewhere, and on the shoulders of a living man!"

"And so have I," said Hilda. "It was what struck me from the first."

"Donatello, look at this face!" cried Kenyon.

The young Italian, as may be supposed, took little interest in matters of art, and seldom or never ventured an opinion respecting them. After holding the sketch a single instant in his hand, he flung it from him with a shudder of disgust and repugnance, and a frown that had all the bitterness of hatred.

"I know the face well!" whispered he. "It is Miriam's model!"

It was acknowledged both by Kenyon and Hilda that they had detected, or fancied, the resemblance which Donatello so strongly affirmed; and it added not a little to the grotesque and weird character which, half playfully, half seriously, they assigned to Miriam's attendant, to think of him as personating the demon's part in a picture of more than two centuries ago. Had

Guido, in his effort to imagine the utmost of sin and misery, which his pencil could represent, hit ideally upon just this face? Or was it an actual portrait of somebody that haunted the old master, as Miriam was haunted now? Did the ominous shadow follow him through all the sunshine of his earlier career, and into the gloom that gathered about its close? And when Guido died, did the spectre betake himself to those ancient sepulchres, there awaiting a new victim, till it was Miriam's illhap to encounter him?

"I do not acknowledge the resemblance at all," said Miriam, looking narrowly at the sketch; "and, as I have drawn the face twenty times, I think you will own that I am the best judge."

A discussion here arose, in reference to Guido's Archangel, and it was agreed that these four friends should visit the Church of the Cappuccini the next morning, and critically examine the picture in question; the similarity between it and the sketch being, at all events, a very curious circumstance.

It was now a little past ten o'clock, when some of the company, who had been standing in a balcony, declared the moonlight to be resplendent. They proposed a ramble through the streets, taking in their way some of those scenes of ruin, which produced their best effects under the splendour of the Italian moon.

CHAPTER XVI.

A Moonlight Ramble.

The proposal for a moonlight ramble was received with acclamation by all the younger portion of the company. They immediately set forth and descended from story to story, dimly lighting their way by waxen tapers, which are a necessary equipment to those whose thoroughfare, in the night-time, lies up and down a Roman staircase. Emerging from the court-yard of the edifice, they looked upward and saw the sky full of light, which seemed to have a delicate purple or crimson lustre, or, at least, some richer tinge than the cold, white moonshine of other skies. It gleamed over the front of the opposite palace, showing the architectural ornaments of its cornice and pillared portal, as well as the iron-barred basement windows, that gave such a prison-like aspect to the structure, and the shabbiness and squalor that lay along its base. A cobbler was just shutting up his little shop, in the basement of the palace; a cigar vendor's lantern flared in the blast that came through the archway; a French sentinel paced to and fro before the portal; a homeless dog, that haunted thereabouts, barked as obstreperously at the party as if he were the domestic guardian of the precincts.

The air was quietly full of the noise of falling water, the cause of which was nowhere visible, though apparently near at hand. This pleasant, natural sound, not unlike that of a distant cascade in the forest, may be heard in many of the Roman streets and piazzas, when the tumult at the city is hushed; for consuls, emperors, and popes, the great men of every age, have found no better way of immortalizing their memories, than by the shifting, indestructible, ever new, yet unchanging, up-gush and downfall of water. They have written their names in that unstable element, and proved it a more durable record than brass or marble.

"Donatello, you had better take one of those gay, boyish artists for your companion," said Miriam, when she found the Italian youth at her side. "I am not now in a merry mood, as when we set all the world a-dancing the other afternoon, in the Borghese grounds."

"I never wish to dance any more," answered Donatello.

"What a melancholy was in that tone!" exclaimed Miriam. "You are getting spoilt, in this dreary Rome, and will be as wise and as wretched as all the rest of mankind, unless you go back soon to your Tuscan vineyards. Well; give me your arm then! But take care that no friskiness comes over you. We must walk evenly and heavily to-night!"

The party arranged itself according to its natural affinities or casual likings; a sculptor generally choosing a painter, and a painter a sculptor, for his companion, in preference to brethren of their own art. Kenyon would gladly have taken Hilda to himself, and have drawn her a little aside from the throng of merry wayfarers. But she kept near Miriam, and seemed, in her gentle and quiet way, to decline a separate alliance either with him or any other of her acquaintances.

So they set forth, and had gone but a little way, when the narrow street emerged into a piazza, on one side of which, glistening, and dimpling in the moonlight, was the most famous fountain in Rome. Its murmur—not to say its uproar—had been in the ears of the company, ever since they came into the open air. It was the Fountain of Trevi, which draws its precious water from a source far beyond the walls, whence it flows hitherward through old subterranean aqueducts, and sparkles forth as pure as the virgin who first led Agrippa to its wellspring, by her father's door.

"I shall sip as much of this water as the hollow of my hand will hold," said Miriam. "I am leaving Rome in a few days; and the tradition goes, that a parting draught at the Fountain of Trevi ensures the traveller's return, whatever obstacles and improbabilities may seem to beset him. Will you drink, Donatello?"

"Signorina, what you drink, I drink," said the youth.

They, and the rest of the party, descended some steps to the water's brim, and, after a sip or two, stood gazing at the absurd design of the fountain, where some sculptor of Bernini's school had gone absolutely mad, in marble. It was a great palace-front, with niches and many bas-reliefs, out of which looked Agrippa's legendary virgin, and several of the allegoric sisterhood; while, at the base, appeared Neptune, with his floundering steeds and Tritons blowing their horns about him, and twenty other artificial fantasies, which the calm moonlight soothed into better taste than was native to them.

And, after all, it was as magnificent a piece of work as ever human skill contrived. At the foot of the palatial façade, was strown, with careful art and ordered irregularity, a broad and broken heap of massive rock, looking as if it might have lain there since the deluge. Over a central precipice fell the water, in a semicircular cascade; and from a hundred crevices, on all sides, snowy jets gushed up, and streams spouted out of the mouths and nostrils of stone monsters, and fell in glistening drops; while other rivulets, that had run wild, came leaping from one rude step to another, over stones that were mossy, slimy, and green with sedge, because, in a century of their wild play, Nature had adopted the Fountain of Trevi, with all its elaborate devices, for her own. Finally, the water, tumbling, sparkling, and dashing, with joyous haste and never-ceasing murmur, poured itself into a great marble-brimmed reservoir, and filled it with a quivering tide; on which was seen, continually, a snowy semicircle of momentary foam from the principal cascade, as well as a multitude of snow-points from smaller jets. The basin occupied the whole breadth of the piazza,

whence flights of steps descended to its border. A boat might float, and make voyages from one shore to another, in this mimic lake.

In the daytime, there is hardly a livelier scene in Rome than the neighbourhood of the Fountain of Trevi; for the piazza is then filled with the stalls of vegetable and fruit dealers, chesnut roasters, cigar vendors, and other people, whose petty and wandering traffic is transacted in the open air. It is likewise thronged with idlers, lounging over the iron railing, and with Forestieri, who come hither to see the famous fountain. Here, also, are seen men with buckets, urchins with cans, and maidens (a picture as old as the patriarchal times) bearing their pitchers upon their heads. For the water of Trevi is in request, far and wide, as the most refreshing draught for feverish lips, the pleasantest to mingle with wine, and the wholesomest to drink, in its native purity, that can anywhere be found. But, now, at nearly midnight, the piazza was a solitude; and it was a delight to behold this untameable water, sporting by itself in the moonshine, and compelling all the elaborate trivialities of art to assume a natural aspect, in accordance with its own powerful simplicity.

"What would be done with this water-power," suggested an artist, "if we had it in one of our American cities? would they employ it to turn the machinery of a cotton-mill, I wonder?"

"The good people would pull down those rampant marble deities," said Kenyon, "and possibly they would give me a commission to carve the one-and-thirty (is that the number?) sister States, each pouring a silver stream from a separate can into one vast basin, which should represent the grand reservoir of national prosperity."

"Or, if they wanted a bit of satire," remarked an English artist, "you could set those same one-and-thirty States to cleansing the national flag of any stains that it may have incurred. The Roman washerwomen at the lavatory yonder, plying their labour in the open air, would serve admirably as models."

"I have often intended to visit this fountain by moonlight," said Miriam, "because it was here that the interview took place between Corinne and Lord Neville, after their separation and temporary estrangement. Pray come behind me, one of you, and let me try whether the face can be recognized in the water."

Leaning over the stone-brim of the basin, she heard footsteps stealing behind her, and knew that somebody was looking over her shoulder. The moonshine fell directly behind Miriam, illuminating the palace-front and the whole scene of statues and rocks, and filling the basin, as it were, with tremulous and palpable light. Corinne, it will be remembered, knew Lord Neville by the reflection of his face in the water. In Miriam's case, however (owing to the agitation of the water, its transparency, and the angle at which she was compelled to lean over), no reflected image appeared; nor, from the same causes, would it have been possible for the recognition between Corinne and her lover to take place. The moon, indeed, flung Miriam's shadow at the bottom of the basin, as well as two more shadows of persons who had followed her, on either side.

"Three shadows!" exclaimed Miriam. "Three separate shadows, all so black and heavy that they sink in the water! There they lie on the bottom, as if all three were drowned together. This shadow on my right is Donatello; I know him by his curls, and the turn of his head. My left-hand companion puzzles me; a shapeless mass, as indistinct as the premonition of calamity! Which of you can it be? Ah!"

She had turned round, while speaking, and saw beside her the strange creature, whose attendance on her was already familiar, as a marvel and a jest, to the whole company of artists. A general burst of laughter followed the recognition; while the model leaned towards Miriam, as she shrank from him, and muttered something that was inaudible to those who witnessed the scene. By his gestures, however, they concluded that he was inviting her to bathe her hands.

"He cannot be an Italian; at least, not a Roman," observed an artist. "I never knew one of them to care about ablution. See him now! It is as if he were trying to wash off the time-stains and earthly soil of a thousand years!"

Dipping his hands into the capacious wash-bowl before him, the model rubbed them together with the utmost vehemence. Ever and anon, too, he peeped into the water, as if expecting to see the whole Fountain of Trevi turbid with the results of his ablution.

Miriam looked at him, some little time, with an aspect of real terror, and even imitated him by leaning over to peep into the basin. Recovering herself, she took up some of the water in the hollow of her hand, and practised an old form of exorcism by flinging it in her persecutor's face.

"In the name of all the Saints," cried she, "vanish, Demon, and let me be free of you, now and for ever!"

"It will not suffice," said some of the mirthful party, "unless the Fountain of Trevi gushes with holy water."

In fact, the exorcism was quite ineffectual upon the pertinacious demon, or whatever the apparition might be. Still he washed his brown, bony talons; still he peered into the vast basin, as if all the water of that great drinking-cup of Rome must needs be stained black or sanguine; and still he gesticulated to Miriam to follow his example. The spectators laughed loudly, but yet with a kind of constraint; for the creature's aspect was strangely repulsive and hideous.

Miriam felt her arm seized violently by Donatello. She looked at him, and beheld a tiger-like fury gleaming from his wild eyes.

"Bid me drown him!" whispered he, shuddering between rage and horrible disgust. "You shall hear his death gurgle in another instant!"

"Peace, peace, Donatello!" said Miriam, soothingly; for this naturally gentle and sportive being seemed all aflame with animal rage. "Do him no mischief! He is mad; and we are as mad as he, if we suffer ourselves to be disquieted by his antics. Let us leave him to bathe his hands till the fountain run dry, if he find solace and pastime in it. What is it to you or me, Donatello? There, there! Be quiet, foolish boy!"

Her tone and gesture were such as she might have used in taming down the wrath of a faithful hound, that had taken upon himself to avenge some supposed affront to his mistress. She smoothed the young man's curls (for his fierce and sudden fury seemed to bristle among his hair), and touched his cheek with her soft palm, till his angry mood was a little assuaged.

"Signorina, do I look as when you first knew me?" asked he, with a heavy, tremulous sigh, as they went onward, somewhat apart from their companions. "Methinks there has been a change upon me, these many months; and more and more, these last few days. The joy is gone out of my life; all gone! all gone! Feel my hand! Is it not very hot? Ah; and my heart burns hotter still!"

"My poor Donatello, you are ill!" said Miriam, with deep sympathy and pity. "This melancholy and sickly Rome is stealing away the rich, joyous life that belongs to you. Go back, my dear friend, to your home among the hills, where (as I gather from what you have told me) your days were filled with simple and blameless delights. Have you found aught in the world that is worth what you there enjoyed? Tell me truly, Donatello!"

"Yes!" replied the young man.

"And what, in Heaven's name?" asked she.

"This burning pain in my heart," said Donatello; "for you are in the midst of it."

By this time, they had left the Fountain of Trevi considerably behind them. Little further allusion was made to the scene at its margin; for the party regarded Miriam's persecutor as diseased in his wits, and were hardly to be surprised by any eccentricity in his deportment.

Threading several narrow streets, they passed through the Piazza of the Holy Apostles, and soon came to Trajan's forum. All over the surface of what once was Rome, it seems to be the effort of Time to bury up the ancient city, as if it were a corpse, and he the sexton; so that, in eighteen centuries, the soil over its grave has grown very deep, by the slow scattering of dust, and the accumulation of more modern decay upon older ruin.

This was the fate, also, of Trajan's forum, until some papal antiquary, a few hundred years ago, began to hollow it out again, and disclosed the full height of the gigantic column, wreathed round with bas-reliefs of the old Emperor's warlike deeds. In the area before it, stands a grove of stone, consisting of the broken and unequal shafts of a vanished temple, still keeping a majestic order, and apparently incapable of further demolition. The modern edifices of the piazza (wholly built, no doubt, out of the spoil of its old magnificence) look down into the hollow space whence these pillars rise.

One of the immense gray granite shafts lay in the piazza, on the verge of the area. It was a great, solid fact of the Past, making old Rome actually sensible to the touch and eye; and no study of history, nor force of thought, nor magic of song, could so vitally assure us that Rome once existed, as this sturdy specimen of what its rulers and people wrought.

"And, see!" said Kenyon, laying his hand upon it, "there is still a polish remaining on the hard substance of the pillar; and even now, late as it is, I can feel very sensibly the warmth of the noon-day sun, which did its best to heat it through. This shaft will endure for ever! The polish of eighteen centuries ago, as yet but half rubbed off, and the heat of to-day's sunshine, lingering into the night, seem almost equally ephemeral in relation to it."

"There is comfort to be found in the pillar," remarked Miriam, "hard and heavy as it is. Lying here for ever, as it will, it makes all human trouble appear but a momentary annoyance."

"And human happiness as evanescent too," observed Hilda, sighing; "and beautiful art hardly less so! I do not love to think that this dull stone, merely by its massiveness, will last infinitely longer than any picture, in spite of the spiritual life that ought to give it immortality!"

"My poor little Hilda," said Miriam, kissing her compassionately, "would you sacrifice this greatest mortal consolation, which we derive from the transitoriness of all things—from the right of saying, in every conjuncture, 'This, too, will pass away'—would you give up this unspeakable boon, for the sake of making a picture eternal?"

Their moralizing strain was interrupted by a demonstration from the rest of the party, who, after talking and laughing together, suddenly joined their voices, and shouted at full pitch,—

"Trajan! Trajan!"

"Why do you deafen us with such an uproar?" inquired Miriam.

In truth, the whole piazza had been filled with their idle vociferation; the echoes from the surrounding houses reverberating the cry of "Trajan," on all sides; as if there was a great search for that imperial personage, and not so much as a handful of his ashes to be found.

"Why, it was a good opportunity to air our voices in this resounding piazza," replied one of the artists. "Besides, we had really some hopes of summoning Trajan to look at his column, which, you know, he never saw in his lifetime. Here is your model (who, they say, lived and sinned before Trajan's death) still wandering about Rome; and why not the Emperor Trajan?"

"Dead emperors have very little delight in their columns, I am afraid," observed Kenyon. "All that rich sculpture of Trajan's bloody warfare, twining from the base of the pillar to its capital, may be but an ugly spectacle for his ghostly eyes, if he considers that this huge, storied shaft must be laid before the judgment-seat, as a piece of the evidence of what he did in the flesh. If ever I am employed to sculpture a hero's monument, I shall think of this, as I put in the bas-reliefs of the pedestal!"

"There are sermons in stones," said Hilda, thoughtfully smiling at Kenyon's morality; "and especially in the stones of Rome."

The party moved on, but deviated a little from the straight way, in order to glance at the ponderous remains of the Temple of Mars Ultor, within which a convent of nuns is now established,—a dovecote, in the war-god's mansion. At only a little distance, they passed the portico of a Temple of Minerva, most rich and beautiful in architecture, but wofully gnawed by time and shattered by violence, besides being buried midway in the accumulation of soil, that rises over dead Rome like a flood-tide. Within this edifice of antique sanctity, a baker's shop was now established, with an entrance on one side; for, everywhere, the remnants of old grandeur and divinity have been made available for the meanest necessities of to-day.

"The baker is just drawing his loaves out of the oven," remarked Kenyon. "Do you smell how sour they are? I should fancy that Minerva (in revenge for the desecration of her temple) had slily poured vinegar into the batch, if I did not know that the modern Romans prefer their bread in the acetous fermentation."

They turned into the Via Alessandria, and thus gained the rear of the Temple of Peace, and passing beneath its great arches, pursued their way along a hedge-bordered lane. In all probability, a stately Roman street lay buried beneath that rustic-looking pathway; for they had now emerged from the close and narrow avenues of the modern city, and were treading on a soil where the seeds of antique grandeur had not yet produced the squalid crop that elsewhere sprouts from them. Grassy as the lane was, it skirted along heaps of shapeless ruin, and the bare site of the vast temple that Hadrian planned and built. It terminated on the edge of a somewhat abrupt descent, at the foot of which, with a muddy ditch between, rose, in the bright moonlight, the great curving wall and multitudinous arches of the Coliseum.

CHAPTER XVII.

Miriam's Trouble.

As usual of a moonlight evening, several carriages stood at the entrance of this famous ruin, and the precincts and interior were anything but a solitude. The French sentinel on duty beneath the principal archway eyed our party curiously, but offered no obstacle to their admission. Within, the moonlight filled and flooded the great empty space; it glowed upon tier above tier of ruined, grass-grown arches, and made them even too distinctly visible. The splendour of the revelation took away that inestimable effect of dimness and mystery by which the imagination might be assisted to build a grander structure than the Coliseum, and to shatter it with a more picturesque decay. Byron's celebrated description is better than the reality. He beheld the scene in his mind's eye, through the witchery of many intervening years, and faintly illuminated it as if with starlight instead of this broad glow of moonshine.

The party of our friends sat down, three or four of them on a prostrate column, another on a shapeless lump of marble, once a Roman altar; others on the steps of one of the Christian shrines. Goths and barbarians though they were, they chatted as gaily together as if they belonged to the gentle and pleasant race of people who now inhabit Italy. There was much pastime and gaiety just then in the area of the Coliseum, where so many gladiators and wild beasts had fought and died, and where so much blood of Christian martyrs had been lapt up by that fiercest of wild beasts, the Roman populace of yore. Some youths and maidens were running merry races across the open space, and playing at hide-and-seek a little way within the duskiness of the ground-tier of arches, whence now and then you could hear the half-shriek, half-laugh of a frolicksome girl, whom the shadow had betrayed into a young man's arms. Elder groups were seated on the fragments of pillars and blocks of marble that lay round the verge of the arena, talking in the quick, short ripple of the Italian tongue. On the steps of the great black cross in the centre of the Coliseum, sat a party singing scraps of songs, with much laughter and merriment between the stanzas.

It was a strange place for song and mirth. That black cross marks one of the special blood-spots of the earth, where thousands of times over the dying gladiator fell, and more of human agony has been endured for the mere pastime of the multitude than on the breadth of many battle-fields. From all this crime and suffering, however, the spot has derived a more than common sanctity. An inscription promises seven years' indulgence, seven years of remission from the pains of purgatory, and earlier enjoyment of heavenly bliss, for each separate kiss imprinted on the black cross. What

better use could be made of life, after middle-age, when the accumulated sins are many and the remaining temptations few, than to spend it all in kissing the black cross of the Coliseum!

Besides its central consecration, the whole area has been made sacred by a range of shrines, which are erected round the circle, each commemorating some scene or circumstance of the Saviour's passion and suffering. In accordance with an ordinary custom, a pilgrim was making his progress from shrine to shrine upon his knees, and saying a penitential prayer at each. Lightfooted girls ran across the path along which he crept, or sported with their friends close by the shrines where he was kneeling. The pilgrim took no heed, and the girls meant no irreverence; for in Italy religion jostles along side by side with business and sport, after a fashion of its own, and people are accustomed to kneel down and pray, or see others praying between two fits of merriment, or between two sins.

To make an end of our description, a red twinkle of light was visible amid the breadth of shadow that fell across the upper part of the Coliseum. Now it glimmered through a line of arches, or threw a broader gleam as it rose out of some profound abyss of ruin; now it was muffled by a heap of shrubbery which had adventurously clambered to that dizzy height; and so the red light kept ascending to loftier and loftier ranges of the structure until it stood like a star where the blue sky rested against the Coliseum's topmost wall.

It indicated a party of English or Americans paying the inevitable visit by moonlight, and exalting themselves with raptures that were Byron's, not their own.

Our company of artists sat on the fallen column, the pagan altar, and the steps of the Christian shrine, enjoying the moonlight and shadow, the present gaiety and the gloomy reminiscences of the scene, in almost equal share. Artists, indeed, are lifted by the ideality of their pursuits a little way off the earth, and are therefore able to catch the evanescent fragrance that floats in the atmosphere of life above the heads of the ordinary crowd. Even if they seem endowed with little imagination individually, yet there is a property, a gift, a talisman, common to their class, entitling them to partake somewhat more bountifully than other people in the thin delights of moonshine and romance.

"How delightful this is!" said Hilda; and she sighed for very pleasure.

"Yes," said Kenyon, who sat on the column, at her side. "The Coliseum is far more delightful, as we enjoy it now, than when eighty thousand persons sat squeezed together, row above row, to see their fellow-creatures torn by lions and tigers limb from limb. What a strange thought that the Coliseum was really built for us, and has not come to its best uses till almost two thousand years after it was finished!"

"The Emperor Vespasian scarcely had us in his mind," said Hilda, smiling; "but I thank him none the less for building it."

"He gets small thanks, I fear, from the people whose bloody instincts he pampered," rejoined Kenyon. "Fancy a nightly assemblage of eighty thousand melancholy and remorseful ghosts, looking down from those tiers of broken arches, striving to repent of the savage pleasures which they once enjoyed, but still longing to enjoy them over again."

"You bring a Gothic horror into this peaceful moonlight scene," said Hilda.

"Nay, I have good authority for peopling the Coliseum with phantoms," replied the sculptor. "Do you remember that veritable scene in Benvenuto Cellini's autobiography, in which a necromancer of his acquaintance draws a magic circle — just where the black cross stands now, I suppose — and raises myriads of demons? Benvenuto saw them with his own eyes — giants, pigmies, and other creatures of frightful aspect — capering and dancing on yonder walls. Those spectres must have been Romans, in their lifetime, and frequenters of this bloody amphitheatre."

"I see a spectre now!" said Hilda, with a little thrill of uneasiness. "Have you watched that pilgrim, who is going round the whole circle of shrines, on his knees, and praying with such fervency at every one? Now that he has revolved so far in his orbit, and has the moonshine on his face as he turns towards us, methinks I recognize him!"

"And so do I," said Kenyon. "Poor Miriam! Do you think she sees him?"

They looked round, and perceived that Miriam had

risen from the steps of the shrine and disappeared. She had shrunk back, in fact, into the deep obscurity of an arch that opened just behind them.

Donatello, whose faithful watch was no more to be eluded than that of a hound, had stolen after her, and became the innocent witness of a spectacle that had its own kind of horror. Unaware of his presence, and fancying herself wholly unseen, the beautiful Miriam began to gesticulate extravagantly, gnashing her teeth, flinging her arms wildly abroad, stamping with foot. It was as if she had stepped aside for an instant, solely to snatch the relief of a brief fit of madness. Persons in acute trouble, or labouring under strong excitement, with a necessity for concealing it, are prone to relieve their nerves in this wild way; although, when practicable, they find a more effectual solace in shrieking aloud.

Thus, as soon as she threw off her self-control, under the dusky arches of the Coliseum, we may consider Miriam as a mad woman, concentrating the elements of a long insanity into that instant.

"Signorina! signorina! have pity on me!" cried Donatello, approaching her—"this is too terrible!"

"How dare you look at me!" exclaimed Miriam, with a start; then, whispering below her breath, "men have been struck dead for a less offence!"

"If you desire it, or need it," said Donatello, humbly, "I shall not be loth to die."

"Donatello," said Miriam, coming close to the young man, and speaking low, but still the almost insanity of the moment vibrating in her voice, "if you love yourself, if you desire those earthly blessings, such as you, of all men, were made for; if you would come to a good old age among your olive-orchards and your Tuscan vines, as your forefathers did; if you would leave children to enjoy the same peaceful, happy, innocent life, then flee from me. Look not behind you! Get you gone without another word." He gazed sadly at her, but did not stir. "I tell you," Miriam went on, "there is a great evil hanging over me! I know it; I see it in the sky; I feel it in the air! It will overwhelm me as utterly as if this arch should crumble down upon our heads! It will crush you, too, if you stand at my side! Depart, then; and make the sign of the cross, as your faith bids you, when an evil spirit is nigh. Cast me off, or you are lost for ever."

A higher sentiment brightened upon Donatello's face, than had hitherto seemed to belong to its simple expression and sensuous beauty.

"I will never quit you," he said; "you cannot drive me from you."

"Poor Donatello!" said Miriam, in a changed tone, and rather to herself than him. "Is there no other that seeks me out—follows me—is obstinate to share my affliction and my doom—but only you! They call me beautiful; and I used to fancy that, at my need, I could bring the whole world to my feet. And, lo! here is my utmost need; and my beauty and my gifts have brought me only this poor, simple boy. Half-witted, they call him; and surely fit for nothing but to be happy. And I accept his aid! To-morrow, to-morrow, I will tell him all! Ah! what a sin to stain his joyous nature with the blackness of a woe like mine!"

She held out her hand to him, and smiled sadly as Donatello pressed it to his lips. They were now about to emerge from the depth of the arch; but, just then, the kneeling pilgrim, in his revolution round the orbit of the shrines, had reached the one on the steps of which Miriam had been sitting. There, as at the other shrines, he prayed, or seemed to pray. It struck Kenyon, however — who sat close by, and saw his face distinctly—that the suppliant was merely performing an enjoined penance, and without the penitence that ought to have given it effectual life. Even as he knelt, his eyes wandered, and Miriam soon felt that he had detected her, half hidden as she was within the obscurity of the arch.

"He is evidently a good Catholic, however," whispered one of the party. "After all, I fear we cannot identify him with the ancient pagan who haunts the catacombs."

"The doctors of the Propaganda may have converted him," said another; "they have had fifteen hundred years to perform the task."

The company now deemed it time to continue their ramble. Emerging from a side entrance of the Coliseum, they had on their left the Arch of Constantine, and, above it, the shapeless ruins of the Palace of the Cæsars; portions of which have taken shape anew, in

mediæval convents and modern villas. They turned their faces cityward, and, treading over the broad flagstones of the old Roman pavement, passed through the Arch of Titus. The moon shone brightly enough within it, to show the seven-branched Jewish candlestick, cut in the marble of the interior. The original of that awful trophy lies buried, at this moment, in the yellow mud of the Tiber; and, could its gold of Ophir again be brought to light, it would be the most precious relic of past ages, in the estimation of both Jew and Gentile.

Standing amid so much ancient dust, it is difficult to spare the reader the commonplaces of enthusiasm, on which hundreds of tourists have already insisted. Over this half-worn pavement, and beneath this Arch of Titus, the Roman armies had trodden in their outward march, to fight battles, a world's width away. Returning victorious, with royal captives and inestimable spoil, a Roman triumph, that most gorgeous pageant of earthly pride, had streamed and flaunted in hundred-fold succession over these same flag-stones, and through this yet stalwart archway. It is politic, however, to make few allusions to such a past; nor, if we would create an interest in the characters of our story, is it wise to suggest how Cicero's foot may have stepped on yonder stone, or how Horace was wont to stroll near by, making his footsteps chime with the measure of the ode that was ringing in his mind. The very ghosts of that massive and stately epoch have so much density that the actual people of to-day seem the thinner of the two, and stand more ghost-like by the arches and columns, letting the rich sculpture be discerned through their ill-compacted substance.

The party kept onward, often meeting pairs and groups of midnight strollers like themselves. On such a moonlight night as this, Rome keeps itself awake and stirring, and is full of song and pastime, the noise of which mingles with your dreams, if you have gone betimes to bed. But it is better to be abroad, and take our own share of the enjoyable time; for the languor that weighs so heavily in the Roman atmosphere by day, is lightened beneath the moon and stars.

They had now reached the precincts of the Forum.

CHAPTER XVIII.

On the Edge of a Precipice.

"LET us settle it," said Kenyon, stamping his foot firmly down, "that this is precisely the spot where the chasm opened, into which Curtius precipitated his good steed and himself. Imagine the great, dusky gap, impenetrably deep, and with half-shaped monsters and hideous faces looming upward out of it, to the vast affright of the good citizens who peeped over the brim! There, now, is a subject, hitherto unthought of, for a grim and ghastly story, and, methinks, with a moral as deep as the gulf itself. Within it, beyond a question, there were prophetic visions—intimations of all the future calamities of Rome—shades of Goths and Gauls, and even of the French soldiers of to-day. It was a pity to close it up so soon! I would give much for a peep into such a chasm."

"I fancy," remarked Miriam, "that every person takes a peep into it in moments of gloom and despondency; that is to say, in his moments of deepest insight."

"Where is it, then?" asked Hilda. "I never peeped into it."

"Wait, and it will open for you," replied her friend. "The chasm was merely one of the orifices of that pit of blackness that lies beneath us, everywhere. The firmest substance of human happiness is but a thin crust spread over it, with just reality enough to bear up the illusive stage-scenery amid which we tread. It needs no earthquake to open the chasm. A footstep, a little heavier than ordinary, will serve; and we must step very daintily, not to break through the crust at any moment. By-and-by, we inevitably sink! It was a foolish piece of heroism in Curtius to precipitate himself there, in advance; for all Rome, you see, has been swallowed up in that gulf, in spite of him. The Palace of the Cæsars has gone down thither, with a hollow, rumbling sound of its fragments! All the temples have tumbled into it; and thousands of statues have been thrown after! All the armies and the triumphs have marched into the great chasm, with their martial music playing, as they stept over the brink. All the heroes, the statesmen, and the poets! All piled upon poor Curtius, who thought to have saved them all! I am loth to smile at the self-conceit of that gallant horseman, but cannot well avoid it."

"It grieves me to hear you speak thus, Miriam," said Hilda, whose natural and cheerful piety was shocked by her friend's gloomy view of human destinies. "It seems to me that there is no chasm, nor any hideous emptiness under our feet, except what the evil within us digs. If there be such a chasm, let us bridge it over with good thoughts and deeds, and we shall tread safely to the other side. It was the guilt of Rome, no doubt, that caused this gulf to open; and

Curtius filled it up with his heroic self-sacrifice and patriotism, which was the best virtue that the old Romans knew. Every wrong thing makes the gulf deeper; every right one helps to fill it up. As the evil of Rome was far more than its good, the whole commonwealth finally sank into it, indeed, but of no original necessity."

"Well, Hilda, it came to the same thing at last," answered Miriam, despondingly.

"Doubtless, too," resumed the sculptor (for his imagination was greatly excited by the idea of this wondrous chasm), "all the blood that the Romans shed, whether on battle-fields, or in the Coliseum, or on the cross—in whatever public or private murder—ran into this fatal gulf, and formed a mighty subterranean lake of gore, right beneath our feet. The blood from the thirty wounds in Cæsar's breast flowed hitherward, and that pure little rivulet from Virginia's bosom, too! Virginia, beyond all question, was stabbed by her father, precisely where we are standing."

"Then the spot is hallowed for ever!" said Hilda.

"Is there such blessed potency in bloodshed?" asked Miriam. "Nay, Hilda, do not protest! I take your meaning rightly."

They again moved forward. And still, from the Forum and the Via Sacra, from beneath the arches of the Temple of Peace on one side, and the acclivity of the Palace of the Cæsars on the other, there arose singing voices of parties that were strolling through the moonlight. Thus, the air was full of kindred melodies that encountered one another, and twined themselves into a broad, vague music, out of which no single strain could be disentangled. These good examples, as well as the harmonious influences of the hour, incited our artist-friends to make proof of their own vocal powers. With what skill and breath they had, they set up a choral strain—"Hail, Columbia!" we believe—which those old Roman echoes must have found it exceeding difficult to repeat aright. Even Hilda poured the slender sweetness of her note into her country's song. Miriam was at first silent, being perhaps unfamiliar with the air and burden. But, suddenly, she threw out such a swell and gush of sound, that it seemed to pervade the whole choir of other voices, and then to rise above them all, and become audible in what would else have been the silence of an upper region. That volume of melodious voice was one of the tokens of a great trouble. There had long been an impulse upon her—amounting, at last, to a necessity—to shriek aloud; but she had struggled against it, till the thunderous anthem gave her an opportunity to relieve her heart by a great cry.

They passed the solitary column of Phocas, and looked down into the excavated space, where a confusion of pillars, arches, pavements, and shattered blocks and shafts—the crumbs of various ruin dropt from the devouring maw of Time—stand, or lie, at the base of the Capitoline Hill. That renowned hillock (for it is little more) now rose abruptly above them. The ponderous masonry, with which the hill-side is built up, is as old as Rome itself, and looks likely to endure while the world retains any substance or permanence. It once sustained the Capitol, and now bears up the great pile which the mediæval builders raised on the antique foundation, and that still loftier tower, which looks abroad upon a larger page, of deeper historic interest, than any other scene can show. On the same pedestal of Roman masonry, other structures will doubtless rise, and vanish like ephemeral things.

To a spectator on the spot, it is remarkable that the events of Roman history, and Roman life itself, appear not so distant as the Gothic ages which succeeded them. We stand in the Forum, or on the height of the Capitol, and seem to see the Roman epoch close at hand. We forget that a chasm extends between it and ourselves, in which lie all those dark, rude, unlettered centuries, around the birth-time of Christianity, as well as the age of chivalry and romance, the feudal system, and the infancy of a better civilization than that of Rome. Or, if we remember these mediæval times, they look farther off than the Augustan age. The reason may be, that the old Roman literature survives, and creates for us an intimacy with the classic ages, which we have no means of forming with the subsequent ones.

The Italian climate, moreover, robs age of its reverence, and makes it look newer than it is. Not the Coliseum, nor the tombs of the Appian Way, nor the oldest pillar in the Forum, nor any other Roman ruin, be it as dilapidated as it may, ever give the impression of venerable antiquity which we gather, along with the ivy, from the gray walls of an English abbey or castle. And yet every brick or stone, which we pick up among the former, had fallen, ages before the foundation of the latter was begun. This is owing to the kindliness with which Nature takes an English ruin to her heart, covering it with ivy, as tenderly as Robin Redbreast covered the dead babes with forest leaves. She strives to make it a part of herself, gradually obliterating the handiwork of man, and supplanting it with her own mosses and trailing verdure, till she has won the whole structure back. But, in Italy, whenever man has once hewn a stone, Nature forthwith relinquishes her right to it, and never lays her finger on it again. Age after age finds it bare and naked, in the barren sunshine, and leaves it so. Besides this natural disadvantage, too, each succeeding century, in Rome, has done its best to ruin the very ruins, so far as their picturesque effect is concerned, by stealing away the marble and hewn stone, and leaving only yellow bricks, which never can look venerable.

The party ascended the winding way that leads from the Forum to the Piazza of the Campidoglio on the summit of the Capitoline Hill. They stood awhile to contemplate the bronze equestrian statue of Marcus Aurelius. The moonlight glistened upon traces of the gilding which had once covered both rider and steed; these were almost gone, but the aspect of dignity was still perfect, clothing the figure as it were with an imperial robe of light. It is the most majestic representation of the kingly character that ever the world has seen. A sight of the old heathen Emperor is enough to create an evanescent sentiment of loyalty even in a democratic bosom, so august does he look, so fit to rule, so worthy of man's profoundest homage and obedience, so inevitably attractive of his love. He stretches forth his hand with an air of grand beneficence and unlimited authority, as if uttering a decree from which no appeal was permissible, but in which the obedient subject would find his highest interests consulted; a command that was in itself a benediction.

"The sculptor of this statue knew what a king should be," observed Kenyon, "and knew, likewise, the heart of mankind, and how it craves a true ruler, under whatever title, as a child its father."

"Oh, if there were but one such man as this!" exclaimed Miriam. "One such man in an age, and one in all the world; then how speedily would the strife, wickedness, and sorrow of us poor creatures be relieved. We would come to him with our griefs, whatever they might be—even a poor, frail woman burdened with her heavy heart—and lay them at his feet and never need to take them up again. The rightful king would see to all."

"What an idea of the regal office and duty!" said Kenyon, with a smile. "It is a woman's idea of the whole matter to perfection. It is Hilda's too, no doubt?"

"No," answered the quiet Hilda; "I should never look for such assistance from an earthly king."

"Hilda, my religious Hilda," whispered Miriam,

suddenly drawing the girl close to her, "do you know how it is with me? I would give all I have or hope—my life, oh, how freely—for one instant of your trust in God! You little guess my need of it. You really think, then, that He sees and cares for us?"

"Miriam, you frighten me."

"Hush, hush! do not let them hear you!" whispered Miriam. "I frighten you, you say; for Heaven's sake, how? Am I strange? is there anything wild in my behaviour?"

"Only for that moment," replied Hilda, "because you seemed to doubt God's providence."

"We will talk of that another time," said her friend. "Just now it is very dark to me."

On the left of the Piazza of the Campidoglio, as you face cityward, and at the head of the long and stately flight of steps descending from the Capitoline Hill to the level of lower Rome, there is a narrow lane or passage. Into this the party of our friends now turned. The path ascended a little and ran along under the walls of a palace, but soon passed through a gateway, and terminated in a small paved courtyard. It was bordered by a low parapet.

The spot, for some reason or other, impressed them as exceedingly lonely. On one side was the great height of the palace, with the moonshine falling over it, and showing all the windows barred and shuttered. Not a human eye could look down into the little courtyard, even if the seemingly deserted palace had a tenant. On all other sides of its narrow compass there

was nothing but the parapet, which as it now appeared was built right on the edge of a steep precipice. Gazing from its imminent brow, the party beheld a crowded confusion of roofs spreading over the whole space between them and the line of hills that lay beyond the Tiber. A long, misty wreath just dense enough to catch a little of the moonshine floated above the houses midway towards the hilly line, and showed the course of the unseen river. Far away on the right, the moon gleamed on the dome of St. Peter's as well as on many lesser and nearer domes.

"What a beautiful view of the city!" exclaimed Hilda; "and I never saw Rome from this point before."

"It ought to afford a good prospect," said the sculptor; "for it was from this point—at least we are at liberty to think so, if we choose—that many a famous Roman caught his last glimpse of his native city, and of all other earthly things. This is one of the sides of the Tarpeian Rock. Look over the parapet and see what a sheer tumble there might still be for a traitor, in spite of the thirty feet of soil that have accumulated at the foot of the precipice."

They all bent over, and saw that the cliff fell perpendicularly downward to about the depth, or rather more, at which the tall palace rose in height above their heads. Not that it was still the natural, shaggy front of the original precipice; for it appeared to be cased in ancient stone-work, through which the primeval rock showed its face here and there grimly and doubtfully. Mosses grew on the slight projections, and little shrubs sprouted out of the crevices, but could not much soften the stern aspect of the cliff. Brightly as the Italian moonlight fell a-down the height, it scarcely showed what portion of it was man's work, and what was Nature's, but left it all in very much the same kind of ambiguity and half-knowledge in which antiquarians generally leave the identity of Roman remains.

The roofs of some poor-looking houses which had been built against the base and sides of the cliff, rose nearly midway to the top; but from an angle of the parapet there was a precipitous plunge straight downward into a stone-paved court.

"I prefer this to any other site as having been veritably the Traitor's Leap," said Kenyon, "because it was so convenient to the Capitol. It was an admirable idea of those stern old fellows to fling their political criminals down from the very summit on which stood the Senate House and Jove's temple, emblems of the institutions which they sought to violate. It symbolizes how sudden was the fall in those days from the utmost height of ambition to its profoundest ruin."

"Come, come; it is midnight," cried another artist, "too late to be moralizing here. We are literally dreaming on the edge of a precipice. Let us go home."

"It is time, indeed," said Hilda.

The sculptor was not without hopes that he might be favoured with the sweet charge of escorting Hilda to the foot of her tower. Accordingly, when the party prepared to turn back, he offered her his arm. Hilda at first accepted it; but when they had partly threaded the passage between the little courtyard and the Piazza del Campidoglio, she discovered that Miriam had remained behind.

"I must go back," said she, withdrawing her arm from Kenyon's; "but pray do not come with me. Several times this evening I have had a fancy that Miriam had something on her mind, some sorrow or perplexity, which, perhaps, it would relieve her to tell me about. No, no; do not turn back! Donatello will be a sufficient guardian for Miriam and me."

The sculptor was a good deal mortified, and perhaps a little angry; but he knew Hilda's mood of gentle decision and independence too well not to obey her. He therefore suffered the fearless maiden to return alone.

Meanwhile, Miriam had not noticed the departure of the rest of the company; she remained on the edge of the precipice, and Donatello along with her.

"It would be a fatal fall, still," she said to herself, looking over the parapet, and shuddering as her eye measured the depth. "Yes; surely yes! Even without the weight of an over-burdened heart, a human body would fall heavily enough upon those stones to shake all its joints asunder. How soon it would be over!"

Donatello, of whose presence she was possibly not aware, now pressed closer to her side; and he, too, like Miriam, bent over the low parapet and trembled violently. Yet he seemed to feel that perilous fascination which haunts the brow of precipices, tempting the unwary one to fling himself over for the very horror of the thing, for, after drawing hastily back, he again looked down, thrusting himself out farther than before. He then stood silent a brief space, struggling, perhaps, to make himself conscious of the historic associations of the scene.

"What are you thinking of, Donatello?" asked Miriam.

"Who were they," said he, looking earnestly in her face, "who have been flung over here in days gone by?"

"Men that cumbered the world," she replied. "Men whose lives were the bane of their fellow-creatures. Men who poisoned the air, which is the common breath of all, for their own selfish purposes. There was short work with such men in old Roman times. Just in the moment of their triumph a hand, as of an avenging giant, clutched them, and dashed the wretches down this precipice."

"Was it well done?" asked the young man.

"It was well done," answered Miriam; "innocent persons were saved by the destruction of a guilty one, who deserved his doom."

While this brief conversation passed, Donatello had once or twice glanced aside with a watchful air, just as a hound may often be seen to take sidelong note of some suspicious object, while he gives his more direct attention to something nearer at hand. Miriam seemed now first to become aware of the silence that had followed upon the cheerful talk and laughter of a few moments before. Looking round, she perceived that all her company of merry friends had retired, and Hilda, too, in whose soft and quiet presence she had always an indescribable feeling of security. All gone; and only herself and Donatello left hanging over the brow of the ominous precipice.

Not so, however; not entirely alone! In the basement wall of the palace, shaded from the moon, there was a deep, empty niche, that had probably once contained a statue; not empty, either; for a figure now came forth from it and approached Miriam. She must have had cause to dread some unspeakable evil from this strange persecutor, and to know that this was the very crisis of her calamity; for, as he drew near, such a cold, sick despair crept over her, that it impeded her breath, and benumbed her natural promptitude of thought. Miriam seemed dreamily to remember falling on her knees; but, in her whole recollection of that wild moment, she beheld herself as in a dim show, and could not well distinguish what was done and suffered; no, not even whether she were really an actor and sufferer in the scene.

Hilda, meanwhile, had separated herself from the sculptor, and turned back to rejoin her friend. At a distance, she still heard the mirth of her late companions, who were going down the cityward descent of the Capitoline Hill; they had set up a new stave of melody, in which her own soft voice, as well as the powerful sweetness of Miriam's, was sadly missed.

The door of the little courtyard had swung upon its hinges, and partly closed itself. Hilda (whose native gentleness pervaded all her movements) was quietly opening it, when she was startled, midway, by the noise of a struggle within, beginning and ending all in one breathless instant. Along with it, or closely succeeding it, was a loud, fearful cry, which quivered upward through the air, and sank quivering downward to the earth. Then, a silence! Poor Hilda had looked into the courtyard, and saw the whole quick passage of a deed, which took but that little time to grave itself in the eternal adamant.

CHAPTER XIX.

The Faun's Transformation.

The door of the courtyard swung slowly, and closed itself of its own accord. Miriam and Donatello were now alone there. She clasped her hands, and looked wildly at the young man, whose form seemed to have dilated, and whose eyes blazed with the fierce energy that had suddenly inspired him. It had kindled him into a man; it had developed within him an intelligence which was no native characteristic of the Donatello whom we have heretofore known. But that simple and joyous creature was gone for ever.

"What have you done?" said Miriam, in a horror-stricken whisper.

The glow of rage was still lurid on Donatello's face, and now flashed out again from his eyes.

"I did what ought to be done to a traitor!" he replied. "I did what your eyes bade me do, when I asked them with mine, as I held the wretch over the precipice!"

These last words struck Miriam like a bullet. Could it be so? Had her eyes provoked or assented to this deed? She had not known it. But, alas! looking back into the frenzy and turmoil of the scene just acted, she could not deny—she was not sure whether it might be so, or no—that a wild joy had flamed up in her heart, when she beheld her persecutor in his mortal peril. Was it horror?—or ecstacy?—or both in one? Be the emotion what it might, it had blazed up more madly, when Donatello flung his victim off the cliff, and more and more, while his shriek went quivering downward. With the dead thump upon the stones below, had come an unutterable horror.

"And my eyes bade you do it!" repeated she.

They both leaned over the parapet, and gazed downward as earnestly as if some inestimable treasure had fallen over, and were yet recoverable. On the pavement, below, was a dark mass, lying in a heap, with little or nothing human in its appearance, except that the hands were stretched out, as if they might have clutched, for a moment, at the small square stones. But there was no motion in them, now. Miriam watched the heap of mortality while she could count a hundred, which she took pains to do. No stir; not a finger moved!

"You have killed him, Donatello! He is quite dead!" said she. "Stone dead! Would I were so, too!"

"Did you not mean that he should die?" sternly asked Donatello, still in the glow of that intelligence which passion had developed in him. "There was short time to weigh the matter; but he had his trial in that breath or two, while I held him over the cliff, and his sentence in that one glance, when your eyes responded to mine! Say that I have slain him against your will—say that he died without your whole consent—and, in another breath, you shall see me lying beside him."

"Oh, never!" cried Miriam. "My one, own friend! Never, never, never!"

She turned to him—the guilty, blood-stained, lonely woman—she turned to her fellow-criminal, the youth, so lately innocent, whom she had drawn into her doom. She pressed him close, close to her bosom, with a clinging embrace that brought their two hearts together, till the horror and agony of each was combined into one emotion, and that, a kind of rapture.

"Yes, Donatello, you speak the truth!" said she; "my heart consented to what you did. We two slew yonder wretch. The deed knots us together for time and eternity, like the coil of a serpent!"

They threw one other glance at the heap of death below, to assure themselves that it was there; so like a dream was the whole thing. Then they turned from that fatal precipice, and came out of the courtyard, arm in arm, heart in heart. Instinctively, they were heedful not to sever themselves so much as a pace or two from one another, for fear of the terror and deadly chill that would thenceforth wait for them in solitude. Their deed—the crime which Donatello wrought, and Miriam accepted on the instant—had wreathed itself, as she said, like a serpent, in inextricable links about both their souls, and drew them into one, by its terrible contractile power. It was closer than a marriage-bond.

So intimate, in those first moments, was the union that it seemed as if their new sympathy annihilated all other ties, and that they were released from the chain of humanity; a new sphere, a special law, had been created for them alone. The world could not come near them; they were safe!

When they reached the flight of steps, leading downward from the Capitol, there was a far-off noise of singing and laughter. Swift, indeed, had been the rush of the crisis that was come and gone! This was still the merriment of the party that had so recently been their companions; they recognized the voices which, a little while ago, had accorded and sung in cadence with their own. But they were familiar voices no more; they sounded strangely, and, as it were, out of the depths of space; so remote was all that pertained to the past life of these guilty ones, in the moral seclusion that had suddenly extended itself around them. But how close, and ever closer, did the breadth of the immeasurable waste, that lay between them and all brotherhood or sisterhood, now press them one within the other!

"Oh, friend," cried Miriam, so putting her soul into that word that it took a heavy richness of meaning, and seemed never to have been spoken before. "Oh, friend, are you conscious, as I am, of this companionship that knits our heart-strings together?"

"I feel it, Miriam," said Donatello. "We draw one breath; we live one life!"

"Only yesterday," continued Miriam; "nay, only a

short half-hour ago, I shivered in an icy solitude. No friendship, no sisterhood, could come near enough to keep the warmth within my heart. In an instant, all is changed! There can be no more loneliness!"

"None, Miriam!" said Donatello.

"None, my beautiful one!" responded Miriam, gazing in his face, which had taken a higher, almost an heroic aspect from the strength of passion. "None, my innocent one! Surely, it is no crime that we have committed. One wretched and worthless life has been sacrificed, to cement two other lives for evermore."

"For evermore, Miriam!" said Donatello; "cemented with his blood!"

The young man started at the word which he had himself spoken; it may be that it brought home, to the simplicity of his imagination, what he had not before dreamed of—the ever-increasing loathsomeness of a union that consists in guilt. Cemented with blood, which would corrupt and grow more noisome for ever and for ever, but bind them none the less strictly for that!

"Forget it! Cast it all behind you!" said Miriam, detecting, by her sympathy, the pang that was in his heart. "The deed has done its office, and has no existence any more."

They flung the past behind them, as she counselled, or else distilled from it a fiery intoxication, which sufficed to carry them triumphantly through those first moments of their doom. For, guilt has its moment of rapture too. The foremost result of a broken law is ever an ecstatic sense of freedom. And thus there exhaled upward (out of their dark sympathy, at the base of which lay a human corpse) a bliss, or an insanity, which the unhappy pair imagined to be well worth the sleepy innocence that was for ever lost to them.

As their spirits rose to the solemn madness of the occasion, they went onward—not stealthily, not fearfully—but with a stately gait and aspect. Passion lent them (as it does to meaner shapes) its brief nobility of carriage. They trode through the streets of Rome, as if they, too, were among the majestic and guilty shadows, that, from ages long gone by, have haunted the blood-stained city. And, at Miriam's suggestion, they turned aside, for the sake of treading loftily past the old site of Pompey's forum.

"For there was a great deed done here!" she said—"a deed of blood, like ours! Who knows, but we may meet the high and ever-sad fraternity of Cæsar's murderers, and exchange a salutation?"

"Are they our brethren, now?" asked Donatello.

"Yes; all of them," said Miriam; "and many another, whom the world little dreams of, has been made our brother or our sister, by what we have done within this hour!"

And, at the thought, she shivered. Where, then, was the seclusion, the remoteness, the strange, lonesome Paradise, into which she and her one companion had been transported by their crime? Was there, indeed, no such refuge, but only a crowded thoroughfare and jostling throng of criminals? And was it true, that whatever hand had a blood-stain on it—or had poured out poison—or strangled a babe at its birth—or clutched a grandsire's throat, he sleeping, and robbed him of his few last breaths—had now the right to offer itself in fellowship with their two hands? Too certainly, that right existed. It is a terrible thought, that an individual wrong-doing melts into the great mass of human crime, and makes us—who dreamed only of our own little separate sin—makes us guilty of the whole. And thus Miriam and her lover were not an insulated pair, but members of an innumerable confraternity of guilty ones, all shuddering at each other.

"But not now; not yet," she murmured to herself. "To-night, at least, there shall be no remorse!"

Wandering without a purpose, it so chanced that they turned into a street, at one extremity of which stood Hilda's tower. There was a light in her high chamber; a light, too, at the Virgin's shrine; and the glimmer of these two was the loftiest light beneath the stars. Miriam drew Donatello's arm to make him stop, and while they stood at some distance looking at Hilda's window, they beheld her approach and throw it open. She leaned far forth, and extended her clasped hands towards the sky.

"The good, pure child! She is praying, Donatello," said Miriam, with a kind of simple joy at witnessing the devoutness of her friend. Then her own sin rushed upon her, and she shouted, with the rich strength of her voice, "Pray for us, Hilda; we need it!"

Whether Hilda heard and recognized the voice we cannot tell. The window was immediately closed, and her form disappeared from behind the snowy curtain. Miriam felt this to be a token that the cry of her condemned spirit was shut out of heaven.

CHAPTER XX.

The Burial Chaunt.

THE Church of the Capuchins (where, as the reader may remember, some of our acquaintances had made an engagement to meet) stands a little aside from the Piazza Barberini. Thither, at the hour agreed upon on the morning after the scenes last described, Miriam and Donatello directed their steps. At no time are people so sedulously careful to keep their trifling appointments, attend to their ordinary occupations, and thus put a commonplace aspect on life, as when conscious of some secret that if suspected would make them look monstrous in the general eye.

Yet how tame and wearisome is the impression of all ordinary things in the contrast with such a fact! How sick and tremulous, the next morning, is the spirit that has dared so much, only the night before! How icy cold is the heart, when the fervour, the wild ecstasy of passion has faded away, and sunk down among the dead ashes of the fire that blazed so fiercely, and was fed by the very substance of its life! How faintly does the criminal stagger onward, lacking the impulse of that strong madness that hurried him into guilt, and treacherously deserts him in the midst of it!

When Miriam and Donatello drew near the church,

they found only Kenyon awaiting them on the steps. Hilda had likewise promised to be of the party, but had not yet appeared. Meeting the sculptor, Miriam put a force upon herself and succeeded in creating an artificial flow of spirits, which to any but the nicest observation was quite as effective as a natural one. She spoke sympathizingly to the sculptor on the subject of Hilda's absence, and somewhat annoyed him by alluding in Donatello's hearing to an attachment which had never been openly avowed, though perhaps plainly enough betrayed. He fancied that Miriam did not quite recognize the limits of the strictest delicacy; he even went so far as to generalize, and conclude within himself that this deficiency is a more general failing in woman than in man, the highest refinement being a masculine attribute.

But the idea was unjust to the sex at large, and especially so to this poor Miriam, who was hardly responsible for her frantic efforts to be gay. Possibly, moreover, the nice action of the mind is set ajar by any violent shock, as of great misfortune or great crime, so that the finer perceptions may be blurred thenceforth, and the effect be traceable in all the minutest conduct of life.

"Did you see anything of the dear child after you left us?" asked Miriam, still keeping Hilda as her topic of conversation. "I missed her sadly on my way homeward; for nothing ensures me such delightful and innocent dreams (I have experienced it twenty times) as a talk late in the evening with Hilda."

"So I should imagine," said the sculptor, gravely; "but it is an advantage that I have little or no opportunity of enjoying. I know not what became of Hilda after my parting from you. She was not especially my companion in any part of our walk. The last I saw of her she was hastening back to rejoin you in the courtyard of the Palazzo Caffarelli."

"Impossible!" cried Miriam, starting.

"Then did you not see her again?" inquired Kenyon, in some alarm.

"Not there," answered Miriam, quietly; "indeed, I followed pretty closely on the heels of the rest of the party. But do not be alarmed on Hilda's account: the Virgin is bound to watch over the good child, for the sake of the piety with which she keeps the lamp alight at her shrine. And, besides, I have always felt that Hilda is just as safe in these evil streets of Rome as her white doves when they fly downwards from the tower-top, and run to and fro among the horses' feet. There is certainly a providence or purpose for Hilda, if for no other human creature."

"I religiously believe it," rejoined the sculptor; "and yet my mind would be the easier, if I knew that she had returned safely to her tower."

"Then make yourself quite easy," answered Miriam. "I saw her (and it is the last sweet sight that I remember) leaning from her window midway between earth and sky!"

Kenyon now looked at Donatello.

"You seem out of spirits, my dear friend," he observed. "This languid Roman atmosphere is not the airy wine that you were accustomed to breathe at home. I have not forgotten your hospitable invitation to meet you this summer at your castle among the Apennines. It is my fixed purpose to come, I assure you. We shall both be the better for some deep draughts of the mountain-breezes."

"It may be," said Donatello, with unwonted sombreness; "the old house seemed joyous when I was a child. But as I remember it now it was a grim place, too."

The sculptor looked more attentively at the young man, and was surprised and alarmed to observe how entirely the fine, fresh glow of animal spirits had departed out of his face. Hitherto, moreover, even while he was standing perfectly still, there had been a kind of possible gambol indicated in his aspect. It was quite gone now. All his youthful gaiety, and with it his simplicity of manner, was eclipsed, if not utterly extinct.

"You are surely ill, my dear fellow," exclaimed Kenyon.

"Am I? Perhaps so," said Donatello, indifferently; "I never have been ill, and know not what it may be."

"Do not make the poor lad fancy-sick," whispered Miriam, pulling the sculptor's sleeve. "He is of a nature to lie down and die at once, if he finds himself drawing such melancholy breaths as we ordinary people are enforced to burden our lungs withal. But we must get him away from this old, dreamy, and dreary Rome, where nobody but himself ever thought of being gay. Its influences are too heavy to sustain the life of such a creature."

The above conversation had passed chiefly on the steps of the Cappuccini; and, having said so much, Miriam lifted the leathern curtain that hangs before all church doors in Italy.

"Hilda has forgotten her appointment," she observed, "or else her maiden slumbers are very sound this morning. We will wait for her no longer."

They entered the nave. The interior of the church was of moderate compass, but of good architecture, with a vaulted roof over the nave, and a row of dusky chapels on either side of it instead of the customary side-aisles. Each chapel had its saintly shrine, hung round with offerings; its picture above the altar, although closely veiled, if by any painter of renown; and its hallowed tapers, burning continually, to set alight the devotion of the worshippers. The pavement of the nave was chiefly of marble, and looked old and broken, and was shabbily patched here and there with tiles of brick; it was inlaid, moreover, with tombstones of the mediæval taste, on which were quaintly sculptured borders, figures, and portraits in bas-relief, and Latin epitaphs, now grown illegible by the tread of footsteps over them. The church appertains to a convent of Capuchin monks; and, as usually happens when a reverend brotherhood have such an edifice in charge, the floor seemed never to have been scrubbed or swept, and had as little the aspect of sanctity as a kennel; whereas, in all churches of nunneries, the maiden sisterhood invariably show the purity of their own hearts by the virgin cleanliness and visible consecration of the walls and pavement.

As our friends entered the church, their eyes rested at once on a remarkable object in the centre of the nave. It was either the actual body, or, as might rather have been supposed at first glance, the cunningly wrought waxen face and suitably draped figure of a dead monk. This image of wax or clay-cold reality, whichever it might be, lay on a slightly elevated bier, with three tall candles burning on each side, another tall candle at the head, and another at the foot. There was music, too, in harmony with so funereal a spectacle. From beneath the pavement of the church came the deep, lugubrious strain of a *De Profundis*, which sounded like an utterance of the tomb itself; so dismally did it rumble through the burial-vaults, and ooze up among the flat gravestones and sad epitaphs, filling the church as with a gloomy mist.

"I must look more closely at that dead monk before we leave the church," remarked the sculptor. "In the study of my art, I have gained many a hint from the dead, which the living could never have given me."

"I can well imagine it," answered Miriam. "One clay image is readily copied from another. But let us first see Guido's picture. The light is favourable now."

Accordingly, they turned into the first chapel on the right hand, as you enter the nave; and there they beheld—not the picture, indeed—but a closely drawn curtain. The churchmen of Italy make no scruple of sacrificing the very purpose for which a work of sacred art has been created: that of opening the way for religious sentiment through the quick medium of sight, by bringing angels, saints, and martyrs, down visibly upon earth; of sacrificing this high purpose, and, for aught they know, the welfare of many souls along with it, to the hope of a paltry fee. Every work by an artist of celebrity is hidden behind a veil, and seldom revealed, except to Protestants, who scorn it as an object of devotion, and value it only for its artistic merit.

The sacristan was quickly found, however, and lost no time in disclosing the youthful Archangel, setting his divine foot on the head of his fallen adversary. It was an image of that greatest of future events, which we hope for so ardently,—at least, while we are young, —but find so very long in coming—the triumph of goodness over the evil principle.

"Where can Hilda be?" exclaimed Kenyon. "It is not her custom ever to fail in an engagement; and the present one was made entirely on her account. Except herself, you know, we were all agreed in our recollection of the picture."

"But we were wrong, and Hilda right, as you perceive," said Miriam, directing his attention to the point on which their dispute of the night before had arisen. "It is not easy to detect her astray, as regards any picture on which those clear, soft eyes of hers have ever rested."

"And she has studied and admired few pictures so much as this," observed the sculptor. "No wonder; for there is hardly another so beautiful in the world. What an expression of heavenly severity in the Archangel's face! There is a degree of pain, trouble, and disgust at being brought in contact with sin, even for the purpose of quelling and punishing it; and yet a celestial tranquillity pervades his whole being."

"I have never been able," said Miriam, "to admire this picture nearly so much as Hilda does, in its moral and intellectual aspect. If it cost her more trouble to be good, if her soul were less white and pure, she would be a more competent critic of this picture, and would estimate it not half so high. I see its defects to-day more clearly than ever before."

"What are some of them?" asked Kenyon.

"That Archangel, now," Miriam continued; "how fair he looks, with his unruffled wings, with his unhacked sword, and clad in his bright armour, and that exquisitely fitting sky-blue tunic, cut in the latest Paradisaical mode! What a dainty air of the first celestial society! With what half-scornful delicacy he sets his prettily sandalled foot on the head of his prostrate foe! But, is it thus that virtue looks, the moment after its death-struggle with evil? No, no: I could have told Guido better. A full third of the Archangel's feathers should have been torn from his wings; the rest all ruffled, till they looked like Satan's own! His sword should be streaming with blood, and perhaps broken half way to the hilt; his armour crushed, his robes rent, his breast gory; a bleeding gash on his brow, cutting right across the stern scowl of battle! He should press his foot hard down upon the old serpent, as if his very soul depended upon it, feeling him squirm mightily, and doubting whether the fight were half over yet, and how the victory might turn! And, with all this fierceness, this grimness, this unutterable horror, there should still be something high, tender, and holy, in Michael's eyes, and around his mouth. But the battle never was such child's play as Guido's dapper Archangel seems to have found it."

"For Heaven's sake, Miriam," cried Kenyon, astonished at the wild energy of her talk; "paint the picture of man's struggle against sin according to your own ideal I think it will be a masterpiece."

"The picture would have its share of truth, I assure you," she answered; "but I am sadly afraid the victory would fall on the wrong side. Just fancy a smoke-blackened, fiery-eyed demon, bestriding that nice young angel, clutching his white throat with one of his hinder claws; and giving a triumphant whisk of his scaly tail, with a poisonous dart at the end of it! That is what they risk, poor souls, who do battle with Michael's enemy."

It now, perhaps, struck Miriam that her mental disquietude was impelling her to an undue vivacity; for she paused, and turned away from the picture, without saying a word more about it. All this while, moreover, Donatello had been very ill at ease, casting awe-stricken and inquiring glances at the dead monk; as if he could look nowhere but at that ghastly object, merely because it shocked him. Death has probably a peculiar horror and ugliness, when forced upon the contemplation of a person so naturally joyous as Donatello, who lived with completeness in the present moment, and was able to form but vague images of the future.

"What is the matter, Donatello?" whispered Miriam, soothingly. "You are quite in a tremble, my poor friend! What is it?"

"This awful chaunt from beneath the church," answered Donatello; "it oppresses me; the air is so heavy with it that I can scarcely draw my breath. And yonder dead monk! I feel as if he were lying right across my heart."

"Take courage!" whispered she again, "come; we will approach close to the dead monk. The only way, in such cases, is to stare the ugly horror right in the face; never a side-long glance, nor a half-look, for those are what show a frightful thing in its frightfulest aspect. Lean on me, dearest friend! My heart is very strong for both of us. Be brave; and all is well."

Donatello hung back for a moment, but then pressed close to Miriam's side, and suffered her to lead him up to the bier. The sculptor followed. A number of persons, chiefly women, with several children among them, were standing about the corpse; and as our three friends drew nigh, a mother knelt down, and caused her little boy to kneel, both kissing the beads and crucifix that hung from the monk's girdle. Possibly he had died in the odour of sanctity; or, at all events, death and his brown frock and cowl made a sacred image of this reverend father.

CHAPTER XXI.

The Dead Capuchin.

The dead monk was clad, as when alive, in the brown woollen frock of the Capuchins, with the hood drawn over his head, but so as to leave the features and a portion of the beard uncovered. His rosary and cross hung at his side; his hands were folded over his breast; his feet (he was of a bare-footed order in his lifetime, and continued so in death) protruded from beneath his habit, stiff and stark, with a more waxen look than even his face. They were tied together at the ankles with a black ribbon.

The countenance, as we have already said, was fully displayed. It had a purplish hue upon it, unlike the paleness of an ordinary corpse, but as little resembling the flush of natural life. The eyelids were but partially drawn down, and showed the eyeballs beneath; as if the deceased friar were stealing a glimpse at the bystanders, to watch whether they were duly impressed with the solemnity of his obsequies. The shaggy eyebrows gave sternness to the look.

Miriam passed between two of the lighted candles, and stood close beside the bier.

"My God!" murmured she. "What is this?"

She grasped Donatello's hand, and, at the same

instant, felt him give a convulsive shudder, which she knew to have been caused by a sudden and terrible throb of the heart. His hand, by an instantaneous change, became like ice within hers, which likewise grew so icy, that their insensible fingers might have rattled one against the other. No wonder that their blood curdled; no wonder that their hearts leapt, and paused! The dead face of the monk, gazing at them beneath its half-closed eyelids, was the same visage that had glared upon their naked souls, the past midnight, as Donatello flung him over the precipice.

The sculptor was standing at the foot of the bier, and had not yet seen the monk's features.

"Those naked feet!" said he. "I know not why, but they affect me strangely. They have walked to and fro over the hard pavements of Rome, and through a hundred other rough ways of this life, where the monk went begging for his brotherhood; along the cloisters and dreary corridors of his convent, too, from his youth upward! It is a suggestive idea, to track those worn feet backward through all the paths they have trodden, ever since they were the tender and rosy little feet of a baby, and (cold as they now are) were kept warm in his mother's hand."

As his companions, whom the sculptor supposed to be close by him, made no response to his fanciful musing, he looked up, and saw them at the head of the bier. He advanced thither himself.

"Ha!" exclaimed he.

He cast a horror-stricken and bewildered glance at

Miriam, but withdrew it immediately. Not that he had any definite suspicion, or, it may be, even a remote idea, that she could be held responsible, in the least degree, for this man's sudden death. In truth, it seemed too wild a thought, to connect, in reality, Miriam's persecutor of many past months and the vagabond of the preceding night, with the dead Capuchin of to-day. It resembled one of those unaccountable changes and interminglings of identity, which so often occur among the personages of a dream. But Kenyon, as befitted the professor of an imaginative art, was endowed with an exceedingly quick sensibility, which was apt to give him intimations of the true state of matters that lay beyond his actual vision. There was a whisper in his ear; it said, "Hush!" Without asking himself wherefore, he resolved to be silent as regarded the mysterious discovery which he had made, and to leave any remark or exclamation to be voluntarily offered by Miriam. If she never spoke, then let the riddle be unsolved.

And now occurred a circumstance that would seem too fantastic to be told, if it had not actually happened, precisely as we set it down. As the three friends stood by the bier, they saw that a little stream of blood had begun to ooze from the dead monk's nostrils; it crept slowly towards the thicket of his beard, where, in the course of a moment or two, it hid itself.

"How strange!" ejaculated Kenyon. "The monk died of apoplexy, I suppose, or by some sudden accident, and the blood has not yet congealed."

"Do you consider that a sufficient explanation?" asked Miriam, with a smile from which the sculptor involuntarily turned away his eyes. "Does it satisfy you?"

"And why not?" he inquired.

"Of course, you know the old superstition about this phenomenon of blood flowing from a dead body," she rejoined. "How can we tell but that the murderer of this monk (or, possibly, it may be only that privileged murderer, his physician) may have just entered the church?"

"I cannot jest about it," said Kenyon. "It is an ugly sight!"

"True, true; horrible to see, or dream of!" she replied, with one of those long, tremulous sighs, which so often betray a sick heart by escaping unexpectedly. "We will not look at it any more. Come away, Donatello. Let us escape from this dismal church. The sunshine will do you good."

When had ever a woman such a trial to sustain as this! By no possible supposition could Miriam explain the identity of the dead Capuchin, quietly and decorously laid out in the nave of his convent church, with that of her murdered persecutor, flung heedlessly at the foot of the precipice. The effect upon her imagination was, as if a strange and unknown corpse had miraculously, while she was gazing at it, assumed the likeness of that face, so terrible henceforth in her remembrance. It was a symbol, perhaps, of the deadly iteration with which she was doomed to behold the image of her crime reflected back upon her in a thousand ways, and converting the great, calm face of Nature, in the whole, and in its innumerable details, into a manifold reminiscence of that one dead visage.

No sooner had Miriam turned away from the bier, and gone a few steps, than she fancied the likeness altogether an illusion, which would vanish at a closer and colder view. She must look at it again, therefore, and at once; or else the grave would close over the face, and leave the awful fantasy that had connected itself therewith, fixed ineffaceably in her brain.

"Wait for me, one moment!" she said to her companions. "Only a moment!"

So she went back, and gazed once more at the corpse. Yes; these were the features that Miriam had known so well; this was the visage that she remembered from a far longer date than the most intimate of her friends suspected; this form of clay had held the evil spirit which blasted her sweet youth, and compelled her, as it were, to stain her womanhood with crime. But, whether it were the majesty of death, or something originally noble and lofty in the character of the dead, which the soul had stamped upon the features, as it left them; so it was that Miriam now quailed and shook, not for the vulgar horror of the spectacle, but for the severe, reproachful glance that seemed to come from between those half-closed lids. True, there had been nothing, in his lifetime, viler than this man. She knew it; there was no other fact within her consciousness that she felt to be so certain;

and yet, because her persecutor found himself safe and irrefutable in death, he frowned upon his victim, and threw back the blame on her!

"Is it thou, indeed?" she murmured, under her breath. "Then thou hast no right to scowl upon me so! But art thou real, or a vision?"

She bent down over the dead monk, till one of her rich curls brushed against his forehead. She touched one of his folded hands with her finger.

"It is he!" said Miriam. "There is the scar, that I know so well, on his brow. And it is no vision; he is palpable to my touch! I will question the fact no longer, but deal with it as I best can."

It was wonderful to see how the crisis developed in Miriam its own proper strength, and the faculty of sustaining the demands which it made upon her fortitude. She ceased to tremble; the beautiful woman gazed sternly at her dead enemy, endeavouring to meet and quell the look of accusation that he threw from between his half-closed eyelids.

"No; thou shalt not scowl me down!" said she. "Neither now, nor when we stand together at the judgment-seat. I fear not to meet thee there. Farewell, till that next encounter!"

Haughtily waving her hand, Miriam rejoined her friends, who were awaiting her at the door of the church. As they went out, the sacristan stopped them, and proposed to show the cemetery of the convent, where the deceased members of the fraternity are laid to rest in sacred earth, brought long ago from Jerusalem.

"And will yonder monk be buried there?" she asked.

"Brother Antonio?" exclaimed the sacristan. "Surely, our good brother will be put to bed there! His grave is already dug, and the last occupant has made room for him. Will you look at it, signorina?"

"I will!" said Miriam.

"Then excuse me," observed Kenyon; "for I shall leave you. One dead monk has more than sufficed me; and I am not bold enough to face the whole mortality of the convent."

It was easy to see, by Donatello's looks, that he, as well as the sculptor, would gladly have escaped a visit to the famous cemetery of the Cappuccini. But Miriam's nerves were strained to such a pitch, that she anticipated a certain solace and absolute relief in passing from one ghastly spectacle to another of long-accumulated ugliness; and there was, besides, a singular sense of duty which impelled her to look at the final resting-place of the being whose fate had been so disastrously involved with her own. She therefore followed the sacristan's guidance, and drew her companion along with her, whispering encouragement as they went.

The cemetery is beneath the church, but entirely above ground, and lighted by a row of iron-grated windows without glass. A corridor runs along beside these windows, and gives access to three or four vaulted recesses, or chapels of considerable breadth

and height, the floor of which consists of the consecrated earth of Jerusalem. It is smoothed decorously over the deceased brethren of the convent, and is kept quite free from grass or weeds, such as would grow even in these gloomy recesses, if pains were not bestowed to root them up. But, as the cemetery is small, and it is a precious privilege to sleep in holy ground, the brotherhood are immemorially accustomed, when one of their number dies, to take the longest-buried skeleton out of the oldest grave, and lay the new slumberer there instead. Thus, each of the good friars, in his turn, enjoys the luxury of a consecrated bed, attended with the slight drawback of being forced to get up long before daybreak, as it were, and make room for another lodger.

The arrangement of the unearthed skeletons is what makes the special interest of the cemetery. The arched and vaulted walls of the burial recesses are supported by massive pillars and pilasters made of thigh-bones and skulls; the whole material of the structure appears to be of a similar kind; and the knobs and embossed ornaments of this strange architecture are represented by the joints of the spine, and the more delicate tracery by the smaller bones of the human frame. The summits of the arches are adorned with entire skeletons, looking as if they were wrought most skilfully in bas-relief. There is no possibility of describing how ugly and grotesque is the effect, combined with a certain artistic merit, nor how much perverted ingenuity has been shown in this queer way, nor what a multitude of dead monks, through how many hundred years, must have contributed their bony framework to build up these great arches of mortality. On some of the skulls there are inscriptions, purporting that such a monk, who formerly made use of that particular head-piece, died on such a day and year; but vastly the greater number are piled up undistinguishably into the architectural design like the many deaths that make up the one glory of a victory.

In the side walls of the vaults are niches where skeleton monks sit or stand, clad in the brown habits that they wore in life, and labelled with their names and the dates of their decease. Their skulls (some quite bare, and others still covered with yellow skin, and hair that has known the earth-damps) look out from beneath their hoods, grinning hideously repulsive. One reverend father has his mouth wide open, as if he had died in the midst of a howl of terror and remorse, which perhaps is even now screeching through eternity. As a general thing, however, these frocked and hooded skeletons seem to take a more cheerful view of their position, and try with ghastly smiles to turn it into a jest. But the cemetery of the Capuchins is no place to nourish celestial hopes: the soul sinks forlorn and wretched under all this burden of dusty death; the holy earth from Jerusalem, so imbued is it with mortality, has grown as barren of the flowers of Paradise as it is of earthly weeds and grass. Thank Heaven for its blue sky; it needs a long, upward gaze to give us back our faith. Not here can we feel ourselves immortal, where the very altars in these chapels of horrible consecration are heaps of human bones.

Yet let us give the cemetery the praise that it deserves. There is no disagreeable scent, such as might have been expected from the decay of so many holy persons, in whatever odour of sanctity they may have taken their departure. The same number of living monks would not smell half so unexceptionably.

Miriam went gloomily along the corridor, from one vaulted Golgotha to another, until in the farthest recess she beheld an open grave.

"Is that for him who lies yonder in the nave?" she asked.

"Yes, signorina, this is to be the resting-place of brother Antonio, who came to his death last night," answered the sacristan; "and in yonder niche, you see, sits a brother who was buried thirty years ago, and has risen to give him place."

"It is not a satisfactory idea," observed Miriam, "that you poor friars cannot call even your graves permanently your own. You must lie down in them, methinks, with a nervous anticipation of being disturbed, like weary men who know that they shall be summoned out of bed at midnight. Is it not possible (if money were to be paid for the privilege) to leave brother Antonio—if that be his name—in the occupancy of that narrow grave till the last trumpet sounds?"

"By no means, signorina; neither is it needful or desirable," answered the sacristan. "A quarter of a century's sleep in the sweet earth of Jerusalem is better than a thousand years in any other soil. Our brethren find good rest there. No ghost was ever known to steal out of this blessed cemetery."

"That is well," responded Miriam; "may he whom you now lay to sleep prove no exception to the rule!"

As they left the cemetery she put money into the sacristan's hand to an amount that made his eyes open wide and glisten, and requested that it might be expended in masses for the repose of Father Antonio's soul.

CHAPTER XXII.

The Medici Gardens.

"DONATELLO," said Miriam, anxiously, as they came through the Piazza Barberini, "what can I do for you, my beloved friend? You are shaking as with the cold fit of the Roman fever."

"Yes," said Donatello; "my heart shivers."

As soon as she could collect her thoughts, Miriam led the young man to the gardens of the Villa Medici, hoping that the quiet shade and sunshine of that delightful retreat would a little revive his spirits. The grounds are there laid out in the old fashion of straight paths, with borders of box, which form hedges of great height and density, and are shorn and trimmed to the evenness of a wall of stone, at the top and sides. There are green alleys, with long vistas, overshadowed by ilex-trees; and at each intersection of the paths, the visitor finds seats of lichen-covered stone to repose upon, and marble statues that look forlornly at him, regretful of their lost noses. In the more open portions of the garden, before the sculptured front of the villa, you see fountains and flower-beds, and, in their season, a profusion of roses, from which the genial sun of Italy distils a fragrance, to be scattered abroad by the no less genial breeze.

But Donatello drew no delight from these things. He walked onward in silent apathy, and looked at Miriam with strangely half-awakened and bewildered eyes, when she sought to bring his mind into sympathy with hers, and so relieve his heart of the burden that lay lumpishly upon it.

She made him sit down on a stone bench, where two embowered alleys crossed each other; so that they could discern the approach of any casual intruder, a long way down the path.

"My sweet friend," she said, taking one of his passive hands in both of hers, "what can I say to comfort you?"

"Nothing!" replied Donatello, with sombre reserve. "Nothing will ever comfort me."

"I accept my own misery," continued Miriam, "my own guilt, if guilt it be—and, whether guilt or misery, I shall know how to deal with it. But you, dearest friend, that were the rarest creature in all this world, and seemed a being to whom sorrow could not cling—you, whom I half fancied to belong to a race that had vanished for ever, you only surviving, to show mankind how genial and how joyous life used to be, in some long-gone age—what had you to do with grief or crime?"

"They came to me as to other men," said Donatello, broodingly. "Doubtless I was born to them."

"No, no; they came with me," replied Miriam. "Mine is the responsibility! Alas! wherefore was I born? Why did we ever meet? Why did I not drive you from me, knowing—for my heart foreboded it—that the cloud in which I walked would likewise envelop you!"

Donatello stirred uneasily, with the irritable impatience that is often combined with a mood of leaden despondency. A brown lizard with two tails—a monster often engendered by the Roman sunshine—ran across his foot, and made him start. Then he sat silent awhile, and so did Miriam, trying to dissolve her whole heart into sympathy, and lavish it all upon him, were it only for a moment's cordial.

The young man lifted his hand to his breast, and, intentionally, as Miriam's hand was within his, he lifted that along with it.

"I have a great weight here!" said he.

The fancy struck Miriam (but she drove it resolutely down) that Donatello almost imperceptibly shuddered, while, in pressing his own hand against his heart, he pressed hers there too.

"Rest your heart on me, dearest one!" she resumed. "Let me bear all its weight; I am well able to bear it; for I am a woman, and I love you! I love you, Donatello! Is there no comfort for you in this avowal? Look at me! Heretofore, you have found me pleasant to your sight. Gaze into my eyes! Gaze into my soul! Search as deeply as you may, you can never see half the tenderness and devotion that I henceforth cherish for you. All that I ask, is your acceptance of the utter self-sacrifice (but it shall be no sacrifice, to my great love) with which I seek to remedy the evil you have incurred for my sake!"

All this fervour on Miriam's part; on Donatello's, a heavy silence.

"Oh, speak to me!" she exclaimed. "Only promise me to be, by and by, a little happy!"

"Happy?" murmured Donatello. "Ah, never again! never again!"

"Never? Ah, that is a terrible word to say to me!" answered Miriam. "A terrible word to let fall upon a woman's heart, when she loves you, and is conscious of having caused your misery! If you love me, Donatello, speak it not again. And surely you did love me?"

"I did," replied Donatello, gloomily and absently.

Miriam released the young man's hand, but suffered one of her own to lie close to his, and waited a moment to see whether he would make any effort to retain it. There was much depending upon that simple experiment.

With a deep sigh—as when, sometimes, a slumberer turns over in a troubled dream—Donatello changed his position, and clasped both his hands over his forehead. The genial warmth of a Roman April kindling into May was in the atmosphere around them; but when Miriam saw that involuntary movement and heard that sigh of relief (for so she interpreted it), a shiver ran through her frame, as if the iciest wind of the Apennines were blowing over her.

"He has done himself a greater wrong than I

dreamed of," thought she, with unutterable compassion. "Alas! it was a sad mistake! He might have had a kind of bliss in the consequences of this deed, had he been impelled to it by a love vital enough to survive the frenzy of that terrible moment—mighty enough to make its own law, and justify itself against the natural remorse. But to have perpetrated a dreadful murder (and such was his crime, unless love, annihilating moral distinctions, made it otherwise) on no better warrant than a boy's idle fantasy! I pity him from the very depths of my soul! As for myself, I am past my own or other's pity."

She arose from the young man's side, and stood before him with a sad, commiserating aspect; it was the look of a ruined soul, bewailing, in him, a grief less than what her profounder sympathies imposed upon herself.

"Donatello, we must part," she said, with melancholy firmness. "Yes; leave me! Go back to your old tower, which overlooks the green valley you have told me of, among the Apennines. Then, all that has passed will be recognized as but an ugly dream. For, in dreams, the conscience sleeps, and we often stain ourselves with guilt of which we should be incapable in our waking moments. The deed you seemed to do, last night, was no more than such a dream; there was as little substance in what you fancied yourself doing. Go: and forget it all!"

"Ah, that terrible face!" said Donatello, pressing his hands over his eyes. "Do you call that unreal?"

"Yes; for you beheld it with dreaming eyes," replied Miriam. "It was unreal; and, that you may feel it so, it is requisite that you see this face of mine no more. Once, you may have thought it beautiful; now, it has lost its charm. Yet it would still retain a miserable potency to bring back the past illusion, and, in its train, the remorse and anguish that would darken all your life. Leave me, therefore, and forget me."

"Forget you, Miriam!" said Donatello, roused somewhat from his apathy of despair. "If I could remember you, and behold you, apart from that frightful visage which stares at me over your shoulder, that were a consolation, at least, if not a joy."

"But since that visage haunts you along with mine," rejoined Miriam, glancing behind her, "we needs must part. Farewell, then! But if ever—in distress, peril, shame, poverty, or whatever anguish is most poignant, whatever burden heaviest—you should require a life to be given wholly, only to make your own a little easier, then summon me! As the case now stands between us, you have bought me dear, and find me of little worth. Fling me away, therefore! May you never need me more! But, if otherwise, a wish—almost an unuttered wish—will bring me to you!"

She stood a moment, expecting a reply. But Donatello's eyes had again fallen on the ground, and he had not, in his bewildered mind and overburdened heart, a word to respond.

"That hour I speak of may never come," said Miriam. "So farewell—farewell for ever."

"Farewell," said Donatello.

His voice hardly made its way through the environment of unaccustomed thoughts and emotions which had settled over him like a dense and dark cloud. Not improbably, he beheld Miriam through so dim a medium that she looked visionary; heard her speak only in a thin, faint echo.

She turned from the young man, and, much as her heart yearned towards him, she would not profane that heavy parting by an embrace, or even a pressure of the hand. So soon after the semblance of such mighty love, and after it had been the impulse to so terrible a deed, they parted, in all outward show, as coldly as people part whose whole mutual intercourse has been encircled within a single hour.

And Donatello, when Miriam had departed, stretched himself at full length on the stone bench, and drew his hat over his eyes, as the idle and light-hearted youths of dreamy Italy are accustomed to do, when they lie down in the first convenient shade, and snatch a noonday slumber. A stupor was upon him, which he mistook for such drowsiness as he had known in his innocent past life. But, by and by, he raised himself slowly and left the garden. Sometimes poor Donatello started, as if he heard a shriek; sometimes he shrank back, as if a face, fearful to behold, were thrust close to his own. In this dismal mood, bewildered with the novelty of sin and grief, he had little left of that singular resemblance, on account of which, and for their sport, his three friends had fantastically recognized him as the veritable Faun of Praxiteles.

CHAPTER XXIII.

Miriam and Hilda.

On leaving the Medici Gardens, Miriam felt herself astray in the world; and having no special reason to seek one place more than another, she suffered chance to direct her steps as it would. Thus it happened, that, involving herself in the crookedness of Rome, she saw Hilda's tower rising before her, and was put in mind to climb up to the young girl's eyrie, and ask why she had broken her engagement at the church of the Capuchins. People often do the idlest acts of their lifetime in their heaviest and most anxious moments; so that it would have been no wonder had Miriam been impelled only by so slight a motive of curiosity as we have indicated. But she remembered, too, and with a quaking heart, what the sculptor had mentioned of Hilda's retracing her steps towards the courtyard of the Palazzo Caffarelli in quest of Miriam herself. Had she been compelled to choose between infamy in the eyes of the whole world, or in Hilda's eyes alone, she would unhesitatingly have accepted the former, on condition of remaining spotless in the estimation of her white-souled friend. This possibility, therefore, that Hilda had witnessed the scene of the past night, was unquestionably the cause that drew Miriam to the tower, and made her linger and falter as she approached it.

As she drew near, there were tokens to which her disturbed mind gave a sinister interpretation. Some of her friend's airy family, the doves, with their heads imbedded disconsolately in their bosoms, were huddled in a corner of the piazza; others had alighted on the heads, wings, shoulders, and trumpets of the marble angels which adorned the façade of the neighbouring church; two or three had betaken themselves to the Virgin's shrine; and as many as could find room were sitting on Hilda's window-sill. But all of them, so Miriam fancied, had a look of weary expectation and disappointment—no flights, no flutterings, no cooing murmur; something that ought to have made their day glad and bright, was evidently left out of this day's history. And, furthermore, Hilda's white window-curtain was closely drawn, with only that one little aperture at the side, which Miriam remembered noticing the night before.

"Be quiet," said Miriam to her own heart, pressing her hand hard upon it. "Why shouldst thou throb now?—Hast thou not endured more terrible things than this?"

Whatever were her apprehensions, she would not turn back. It might be—and the solace would be worth a world—that Hilda, knowing nothing of the past night's calamity, would greet her friend with a sunny smile, and so restore a portion of the vital warmth, for lack of which her soul was frozen. But could Miriam, guilty as she was, permit Hilda to kiss her cheek, to clasp her hand, and thus be no longer so unspotted from the world as heretofore?

"I will never permit her sweet touch again," said Miriam, toiling up the staircase, "if I can find strength of heart to forbid it. But, oh! it would be so soothing in this wintry fever-fit of my heart. There can be no harm to my white Hilda in one parting kiss. That shall be all!"

But, on reaching the upper landing-place, Miriam paused, and stirred not again till she had brought herself to an immoveable resolve.

"My lips, my hand, shall never meet Hilda's more," said she.

Meanwhile, Hilda sat listlessly in her painting-room. Had you looked into the little adjoining chamber, you might have seen the slight imprint of her figure on the bed, but would also have detected at once that the white counterpane had not been turned down. The pillow was more disturbed; she had turned her face upon it, the poor child, and bedewed it with some of those tears (among the most chill and forlorn that gush from human sorrow) which the innocent heart pours forth at its first actual discovery that sin is in the world. The young and pure are not apt to find out that miserable truth until it is brought home to them by the guiltiness of some trusted friend. They may have heard much of the evil of the world, and seem to know it, but only as an impalpable theory. In due time, some mortal, whom they reverence too highly, is commissioned by Providence to teach them this direful lesson; he perpetrates a sin; and Adam falls anew, and Paradise, heretofore in unfaded bloom, is lost again, and closed for ever, with the fiery swords gleaming at its gates.

The chair in which Hilda sat was near the portrait of Beatrice Cenci, which had not yet been taken from the easel. It is a peculiarity of this picture, that its profoundest expression eludes a straightforward glance, and can only be caught by side glimpses, or when the eye falls casually upon it; even as if the painted face had a life and consciousness of its own, and, resolving not to betray its secret of grief or guilt, permitted the true tokens to come forth only when it imagined itself unseen. No other such magical effect has ever been wrought by pencil.

Now, opposite the easel hung a looking-glass, in which Beatrice's face and Hilda's were both reflected. In one of her weary, nerveless changes of position, Hilda happened to throw her eyes on the glass, and took in both these images at one unpremeditated glance. She fancied—nor was it without horror—that Beatrice's expression, seen aside and vanishing in a moment, had been depicted in her own face likewise, and flitted from it as timorously.

"Am I, too, stained with guilt?" thought the poor girl, hiding her face in her hands.

Not so, thank Heaven! But, as regards Beatrice's picture, the incident suggests a theory which may account for its unutterable grief and mysterious shadow of guilt, without detracting from the purity which we love to attribute to that ill-fated girl. Who, indeed, can look at that mouth—with its lips half apart, as innocent as a baby's that has been crying—and not pronounce Beatrice sinless! It was the intimate consciousness of her father's sin that threw its shadow over her, and frightened her into a remote and inaccessible region, where no sympathy could come. It was the knowledge of Miriam's guilt, that lent the same expression to Hilda's face.

But Hilda nervously moved her chair, so that the images in the glass should be no longer visible. She now watched a speck of sunshine that came through a shuttered window, and crept from object to object, indicating each with a touch of its bright finger, and then letting them all vanish successively. In like manner, her mind, so like sunlight in its natural cheerfulness, went from thought to thought, but found nothing that it could dwell upon for comfort. Never before had this young, energetic, active spirit known what it is to be despondent. It was the unreality of the world that made her so. Her dearest friend, whose heart seemed the most solid and richest of Hilda's possessions, had no existence for her any more; and in that dreary void, out of which Miriam had disappeared, the substance, the truth, the integrity of life, the motives of effort, the joy of success, had departed along with her.

It was long past noon, when a step came up the staircase. It had passed beyond the limits where there was communication with the lower regions of the palace, and was mounting the successive flights which led only to Hilda's precincts. Faint as the tread was, she heard and recognized it. It startled her into sudden life. Her first impulse was to spring to the door of the studio, and fasten it with lock and bolt. But a second thought made her feel that this would be an unworthy cowardice, on her own part, and also that Miriam—only yesterday her closest friend—had a right to be told, face to face, that thenceforth they must be for ever strangers.

She heard Miriam pause, outside of the door. We have already seen what was the latter's resolve with respect to any kiss or pressure of the hand between Hilda and herself. We know not what became of the resolution. As Miriam was of a highly impulsive character, it may have vanished at the first sight of Hilda; but, at all events, she appeared to have dressed herself up in a garb of sunshine, and was disclosed, as the door swung open, in all the glow of her remarkable beauty. The truth was, her heart leaped convulsively towards the only refuge that it had, or hoped. She forgot, just one instant, all cause for holding herself aloof. Ordinarily there was a certain reserve in Miriam's demonstrations of affection, in consonance with the delicacy of her friend. To-day, she opened her arms to take Hilda in.

"Dearest, darling Hilda!" she exclaimed. "It gives me new life to see you!"

Hilda was standing in the middle of the room. When her friend made a step or two from the door, she put forth her hands with an involuntary repellent gesture, so expressive, that Miriam at once felt a great chasm opening itself between them two. They might gaze at one another from the opposite side, but without the possibility of ever meeting more; or, at least, since the chasm could never be bridged over, they must tread the whole round of Eternity to meet on the other side. There was even a terror in the thought of their meeting again. It was as if Hilda or Miriam were dead, and could no longer hold intercourse without violating a spiritual law.

Yet, in the wantonness of her despair, Miriam made one more step towards the friend whom she had lost.

"Do not come nearer, Miriam!" said Hilda.

Her look and tone were those of sorrowful entreaty, and yet they expressed a kind of confidence, as if the girl were conscious of a safeguard that could not be violated.

"What has happened between us, Hilda?" asked Miriam. "Are we not friends?"

"No, no!" said Hilda, shuddering.

"At least, we have been friends," continued Miriam. "I loved you dearly! I love you still! You were to me as a younger sister; yes, dearer than sisters of the same blood; for you and I were so lonely, Hilda, that the whole world pressed us together by its solitude and strangeness. Then, will you not touch my hand? Am I not the same as yesterday?"

"Alas! no, Miriam!" said Hilda.

"Yes, the same—the same for you, Hilda," rejoined her lost friend. "Were you to touch my hand, you would find it as warm to your grasp as ever. If you were sick or suffering, I would watch night and day for you. It is in such simple offices that true affection shows itself; and so I speak of them. Yet now, Hilda, your very look seems to put me beyond the limits of humankind!"

"It is not I, Miriam," said Hilda; "not I that have done this."

"You, and you only, Hilda," replied Miriam, stirred up to make her own cause good by the repellent force which her friend opposed to her. "I am a woman, as I was yesterday; endowed with the same truth of nature, the same warmth of heart, the same genuine and earnest love, which you have always known in me. In any regard that concerns yourself, I am not changed. And believe me, Hilda, when a human being has chosen a friend out of all the world, it is only some faithlessness between themselves, rendering true intercourse impossible, that can justify either friend in severing the bond. Have I deceived you? Then cast me off! Have I wronged you personally? Then forgive me, if you can. But, have I sinned against God and man, and deeply sinned? Then be more my friend than ever, for I need you more."

"Do not bewilder me thus, Miriam!" exclaimed Hilda, who had not forborne to express, by look and gesture, the anguish which this interview inflicted on her. "If I were one of God's angels, with a nature incapable of stain, and garments that never could be spotted, I would keep ever at your side, and try to lead you upward. But I am a poor, lonely girl, whom God has set here in an evil world, and given her only a white robe, and bid her wear it back to Him, as white as when she put it on. Your powerful magnetism would be too much for me. The pure, white atmosphere, in which I try to discern what things are good and true, would be discoloured. And therefore, Miriam, before it is too late, I mean to put faith in this awful heart-quake, which warns me henceforth to avoid you."

"Ah, this is hard! Ah, this is terrible!" murmured Miriam, dropping her forehead in her hands. In a moment or two she looked up again, as pale as death, but with a composed countenance: "I always said, Hilda, that you were merciless; for I had a perception of it, even while you loved me best. You have no sin, nor any conception of what it is; and therefore you are so terribly severe! As an angel, you are not amiss; but, as a human creature, and a woman among earthly men and women, you need a sin to soften you."

"God forgive me," said Hilda, "if I have said a needlessly cruel word!"

"Let it pass," answered Miriam; "I, whose heart it has smitten upon, forgive you. And tell me, before we part for ever, what have you seen or known of me, since we last met?"

"A terrible thing, Miriam," said Hilda, growing paler than before.

"Do you see it written in my face, or painted in my eyes?" inquired Miriam, her trouble seeking relief in a half-frenzied raillery. "I would fain know how it is that Providence, or fate, brings eye-witnesses to watch us, when we fancy ourselves acting in the remotest privacy. Did all Rome see it, then? Or, at least, our merry company of artists? Or is it some blood-stain on me, or death-scent in my garments? They say that monstrous deformities sprout out of fiends, who once were lovely angels. Do you perceive such in me already? Tell me, by our past friendship, Hilda, all you know."

Thus adjured, and frightened by the wild emotion which Miriam could not suppress, Hilda strove to tell what she had witnessed.

"After the rest of the party had passed on, I went back to speak to you," she said; "for there seemed to be a trouble on your mind, and I wished to share it with you, if you could permit me. The door of the little courtyard was partly shut; but I pushed it open, and saw you within, and Donatello, and a third person, whom I had before noticed in the shadow of a niche. He approached you, Miriam. You knelt to him!—I saw Donatello spring upon him! I would have shrieked, but my throat was dry. I would have rushed forward; but my limbs seemed rooted to the earth.—It was all like a flash of lightning. A look passed from your eyes to Donatello's—a look—"

"Yes, Hilda, yes!" exclaimed Miriam, with intense eagerness. "Do not pause now! That look?"

"It revealed all your heart, Miriam," continued Hilda, covering her eyes as if to shut out the recollection; "a look of hatred, triumph, vengeance, and, as it were, joy at some unhoped-for relief."

"Ah! Donatello was right, then," murmured Miriam, who shook throughout all her frame. "My eyes bade him do it! Go on, Hilda."

"It all passed so quickly—all like a glare of lightning," said Hilda, "and yet it seemed to me that Donatello had paused, while one might draw a breath. But that look!—Ah Miriam, spare me. Need I tell more?"

"No more; there needs no more, Hilda," replied Miriam, bowing her head, as if listening to a sentence of condemnation from a supreme tribunal. "It is enough! You have satisfied my mind on a point where it was greatly disturbed. Henceforward, I shall be quiet. Thank you, Hilda."

She was on the point of departing, but turned back again from the threshold.

"This is a terrible secret to be kept in a young girl's bosom," she observed; "what will you do with it, my poor child?"

"Heaven help and guide me," answered Hilda, bursting into tears; "for the burden of it crushes me to the earth! It seems a crime to know of such a thing, and to keep it to myself. It knocks within my heart continually, threatening, imploring, insisting to be let out! Oh, my mother!—my mother! Were she yet living, I would travel over land and sea to tell her this dark secret, as I told all the little troubles of my infancy. But I am alone—alone! Miriam, you were my dearest, only friend. Advise me what to do."

This was a singular appeal, no doubt, from the stainless maiden to the guilty woman, whom she had just banished from her heart for ever. But it bore striking testimony to the impression which Miriam's natural uprightness and impulsive generosity had made on the friend who knew her best; and it deeply comforted the poor criminal, by proving to her that the bond between Hilda and herself was vital yet.

As far as she was able, Miriam at once responded to the girl's cry for help.

"If I deemed it good for your peace of mind," she said, "to bear testimony against me for this deed, in the face of all the world, no consideration of myself should weigh with me an instant. But I believe that you would find no relief in such a course. What men call justice lies chiefly in outward formalities, and has never the close application and fitness that would be satisfactory to a soul like yours. I cannot be fairly tried and judged before an earthly tribunal; and of this, Hilda, you would perhaps become fatally conscious, when it was too late. Roman justice, above all things, is a byword. What have you to do with it? Leave all such thoughts aside! Yet, Hilda, I would not have you keep my secret imprisoned in your heart, if it tries to leap out, and stings you, like a wild, venomous thing, when you thrust it back again. Have you no other friend, now that you have been forced to give me up?"

"No other," answered Hilda, sadly.

"Yes; Kenyon!" rejoined Miriam.

"He cannot be my friend," said Hilda, "because —because—I have fancied that he sought to be something more."

"Fear nothing!" replied Miriam, shaking her head, with a strange smile. "This story will frighten his new-born love out of its little life, if that be what you wish. Tell him the secret, then, and take his wise and honourable counsel as to what should next be done. I know not what else to say."

"I never dreamed," said Hilda,—"how could you think it?—of betraying you to justice. But I see how it is, Miriam. I must keep your secret, and die of it, unless God sends me some relief by methods which are now beyond my power to imagine. It is very dreadful. Ah! now I understand how the sins of generations past have created an atmosphere of sin for those that follow. While there is a single guilty person in the universe, each innocent one must feel his innocence tortured by that guilt. Your deed, Miriam, has darkened the whole sky!"

Poor Hilda turned from her unhappy friend, and, sinking on her knees in a corner of the chamber, could not be prevailed upon to utter another word. And Miriam, with a long regard from the threshold, bade farewell to this doves' nest, this one little nook of pure thoughts and innocent enthusiasms, into which she had brought such trouble. Every crime destroys more Edens than our own!

CHAPTER XXIV.

The Tower among the Appennines.

It was in June, that the sculptor, Kenyon, arrived on horseback at the gate of an ancient country-house (which, from some of its features, might almost be called a castle) situated in a part of Tuscany somewhat remote from the ordinary track of tourists. Thither we must now accompany him, and endeavour to make our story flow onward, like a streamlet, past a gray tower that rises on the hillside, overlooking a spacious valley, which is set in the grand framework of the Apennines.

The sculptor had left Rome with the retreating tide of foreign residents. For, as summer approaches, the Niobe of Nations is made to bewail anew, and doubtless with sincerity, the loss of that large part of her population, which she derives from other lands, and on whom depends much of whatever remnant of prosperity she still enjoys. Rome, at this season, is pervaded and overhung with atmospheric terrors, and insulated within a charmed and deadly circle. The crowd of wandering tourists betake themselves to Switzerland, to the Rhine, or, from this central home of the world, to their native homes in England or America, which they are apt thenceforward to look upon as provincial, after once having yielded to the spell of the Eternal City. The artist, who contemplates an indefinite succession of winters in this home of art (though his first thought was merely to improve himself by a brief visit), goes forth, in the summer time, to sketch scenery and costume among the Tuscan hills, and pour, if he can, the purple air of Italy over his canvas. He studies the old schools of art in the mountain-towns where they were born, and where they are still to be seen in the faded frescoes of Giotto and Cimabue, on the walls of many a church, or in the dark chapels, in which the sacristan draws aside the veil from a treasured picture of Perugino. Thence, the happy painter goes to walk the long, bright galleries of Florence, or to steal glowing colours from the miraculous works, which he finds in a score of Venetian palaces. Such summers as these, spent amid whatever is exquisite in art, or wild and picturesque in nature, may not inadequately repay him for the chill neglect and disappointment through which he has probably languished, in his Roman winter. This sunny, shadowy, breezy, wandering life, in which he seeks for beauty as his treasure, and gathers for his winter's honey what is but a passing fragrance to all other men, is worth living for, come afterwards what may. Even if he die unrecognized, the artist has had his share of enjoyment and success.

Kenyon had seen, at a distance of many miles, the old villa or castle, towards which his journey lay, looking from its height over a broad expanse of valley.

As he drew nearer, however, it had been hidden among the inequalities of the hill-side, until the winding road brought him almost to the iron gateway. The sculptor found this substantial barrier fastened with lock and bolt. There was no bell, nor other instrument of sound; and, after summoning the invisible garrison with his voice, instead of a trumpet, he had leisure to take a glance at the exterior of the fortress.

About thirty yards within the gateway rose a square tower, lofty enough to be a very prominent object in the landscape, and more than sufficiently massive in proportion to its height. Its antiquity was evidently such, that, in a climate of more abundant moisture, the ivy would have mantled it from head to foot in a garment that might, by this time, have been centuries old, though ever new. In the dry Italian air, however, Nature had only so far adopted this old pile of stone-work as to cover almost every hand's-breadth of it with close-clinging lichens and yellow moss; and the immemorial growth of these kindly productions rendered the general hue of the tower soft and venerable, and took away the aspect of nakedness which would have made its age drearier than now.

Up and down the height of the tower were scattered three or four windows, the lower ones grated with iron bars, the upper ones vacant both of window-frames and glass. Besides these larger openings, there were several loopholes and little square apertures, which might be supposed to light the staircase, that doubtless climbed the interior towards the battlemented and machicolated summit. With this last-mentioned warlike garniture upon its stern old head and brow, the tower seemed evidently a stronghold of times long past. Many a crossbowman had shot his shafts from those windows and loopholes, and from the vantage height of those gray battlements; many a flight of arrows, too, had hit all round about the embrasures above, or the apertures below, where the helmet of a defender had momentarily glimmered. On festal nights, moreover, a hundred lamps had often gleamed afar over the valley, suspended from the iron hooks that were ranged for the purpose beneath the battlements and every window.

Connected with the tower, and extending behind it, there seemed to be a very spacious residence, chiefly of more modern date. It perhaps owed much of its fresher appearance, however, to a coat of stucco and yellow wash, which is a sort of renovation very much in vogue with the Italians. Kenyon noticed over a doorway, in the portion of the edifice immediately adjacent to the tower, a cross, which, with a bell suspended above the roof, indicated that this was a consecrated precinct, and the chapel of the mansion.

Meanwhile, the hot sun so incommoded the unsheltered traveller, that he shouted forth another impatient summons. Happening, at the same moment, to look upward, he saw a figure leaning from an embrasure of the battlements, and gazing down at him.

"Ho, Signor Count!" cried the sculptor, waving his straw hat, for he recognized the face, after a moment's doubt. "This is a warm reception, truly! Pray bid your porter let me in, before the sun shrivels me quite into a cinder."

"I will come myself," responded Donatello, flinging down his voice out of the clouds, as it were; "old Tomaso and old Stella are both asleep no doubt, and the rest of the people are in the vineyard. But I have expected you, and you are welcome!"

The young count—as perhaps we had better designate him in his ancestral tower—vanished from the battlements; and Kenyon saw his figure appear successively at each of the windows, as he descended. On every reappearance, he turned his face towards the sculptor and gave a nod and smile; for a kindly impulse prompted him thus to assure his visitor of a welcome, after keeping him so long at an inhospitable threshold.

Kenyon, however (naturally and professionally expert at reading the expression of the human countenance), had a vague sense that this was not the young friend whom he had known so familiarly in Rome; not the sylvan and untutored youth, whom Miriam, Hilda, and himself, had liked, laughed at, and sported with; not the Donatello whose identity they had so playfully mixed up with that of the Faun of Praxiteles.

Finally, when his host had emerged from a side-portal of the mansion, and approached the gateway, the traveller still felt that there was something lost, or something gained (he hardly knew which), that set the Donatello of to-day irreconcileably at odds with him of yesterday. His very gait showed it, in a certain gravity, a weight and measure of step, that had nothing in common with the irregular buoyancy which used to distinguish him. His face was paler and thinner, and the lips less full, and less apart.

"I have looked for you a long while," said Donatello; and, though his voice sounded differently, and cut out its words more sharply than had been its wont, still there was a smile shining on his face, that, for the moment, quite brought back the Faun. "I shall be more cheerful, perhaps, now that you have come. It is very solitary here."

"I have come slowly along, often lingering, often turning aside," replied Kenyon; "for I found a great deal to interest me in the mediæval sculpture hidden away in the churches hereabouts. An artist, whether painter or sculptor, may be pardoned for loitering through such a region. But what a fine old tower! Its tall front is like a page of black-letter, taken from the history of the Italian republics."

"I know little or nothing of its history," said the count, glancing upward at the battlements, where he had just been standing. "But I thank my forefathers for building it so high. I like the windy summit better than the world below, and spend much of my time there, now-a-days."

"It is a pity you are not a star-gazer," observed Kenyon, also looking up. "It is higher than Galileo's tower, which I saw, a week or two ago, outside of the walls of Florence."

"A star-gazer! I am one," replied Donatello. "I sleep in the tower, and often watch very late on the battlements. There is a dismal old staircase to climb, however, before reaching the top, and a succession of dismal chambers, from story to story. Some of them were prison chambers in times past, as old Tomaso will tell you."

The repugnance intimated in his tone at the idea of this gloomy staircase and these ghostly, dimly lighted rooms, reminded Kenyon of the original Donatello, much more than his present custom of midnight vigils on the battlements.

"I shall be glad to share your watch," said the guest; "especially by moonlight. The prospect of this broad valley must be very fine. But I was not aware, my friend, that these were your country habits. I have fancied you in a sort of Arcadian life, tasting rich figs, and squeezing the juice out of the sunniest grapes, and sleeping soundly, all night, after a day of simple pleasures."

"I may have known such a life, when I was younger," answered the count, gravely. "I am not a boy now. Time flies over us, but leaves its shadow behind."

The sculptor could not but smile at the triteness of the remark, which, nevertheless, had a kind of originality as coming from Donatello. He had thought it out from his own experience, and perhaps considered himself as communicating a new truth to mankind.

They were now advancing up the courtyard; and

the long extent of the villa, with its iron-barred lower windows and balconied upper ones, became visible, stretching back towards a grove of trees.

"At some period of your family history," observed Kenyon, "the Counts of Monte Beni must have led a patriarchal life in this vast house. A great-grandsire and all his descendants might find ample verge here, and with space, too, for each separate brood of little ones to play within its own precincts. Is your present household a large one?"

"Only myself," answered Donatello, "and Tomaso, who has been butler since my grandfather's time, and old Stella, who goes sweeping and dusting about the chambers, and Girolamo, the cook, who has but an idle life of it. He shall send you up a chicken forthwith. But, first of all, I must summon one of the contadini from the farmhouse yonder, to take your horse to the stable."

Accordingly, the young count shouted amain, and with such effect, that, after several repetitions of the outcry, an old gray woman protruded her head and a broom-handle from a chamber window; the venerable butler emerged from a recess in the side of the house, where was a well, or reservoir, in which he had been cleansing a small wine cask; and a sun-burnt contadino, in his shirt-sleeves, showed himself on the outskirts of the vineyard, with some kind of a farming tool in his hand. Donatello found employment for all these retainers in providing accommodation for his guest and steed, and then ushered the sculptor into the vestibule of the house.

It was a square and lofty entrance room, which, by the solidity of its construction, might have been an Etruscan tomb, being paved and walled with heavy blocks of stone, and vaulted almost as massively overhead. On two sides, there were doors, opening into long suites of ante-rooms and saloons; on the third side, a stone staircase, of spacious breadth, ascending, by dignified degrees and with wide resting-places, to another floor of similar extent. Through one of the doors, which was ajar, Kenyon beheld an almost interminable vista of apartments, opening one beyond the other, and reminding him of the hundred rooms in Blue Beard's castle, or the countless halls in some palace of the Arabian Nights.

It must have been a numerous family, indeed, that could ever have sufficed to people with human life so large an abode as this, and impart social warmth to such a wide world within doors. The sculptor confessed to himself, that Donatello could allege reason enough for growing melancholy, having only his own personality to vivify it all.

"How a woman's face would brighten it up!" he ejaculated, not intending to be overheard.

But, glancing at Donatello, he saw a stern and sorrowful look in his eyes, which altered his youthful face as much as if it had seen thirty years of trouble; and, at the same moment, old Stella showed herself through one of the doorways, as the only representative of her sex at Monte Beni.

CHAPTER XXV.

Sunshine.

"Come," said the count, "I see you already find the old house dismal. So do I, indeed! And yet it was a cheerful place in my boyhood. But, you see, in my father's days (and the same was true of all my endless line of grandfathers, as I have heard), there used to be uncles, aunts, and all manner of kindred, dwelling together as one family. They were a merry and kindly race of people, for the most part, and kept one another's hearts warm."

"Two hearts might be enough for warmth," observed the sculptor, "even in so large a house as this. One solitary heart, it is true, may be apt to shiver a little. But, I trust, my friend, that the genial blood of your race still flows in many veins besides your own?"

"I am the last," said Donatello, gloomily. "They have all vanished from me, since my childhood. Old Tomaso will tell you that the air of Monte Beni is not so favourable to length of days as it used to be. But that is not the secret of the quick extinction of my kindred."

"Then you are aware of a more satisfactory reason?" suggested Kenyon.

"I thought of one, the other night, while I was gazing at the stars," answered Donatello; "but, pardon me, I do not mean to tell it. One cause, however, of the longer and healthier life of my forefathers was, that they had many pleasant customs, and means of making themselves glad, and their guests and friends along with them. Now-a-days we have but one!"

"And what is that?" asked the sculptor.

"You shall see!" said his young host.

By this time, he had ushered the sculptor into one of the numberless saloons; and, calling for refreshment, old Stella placed a cold fowl upon the table, and quickly followed it with a savoury omelette, which Girolamo had lost no time in preparing. She also brought some cherries, plums, and apricots, and a plate full of particularly delicate figs, of last year's growth. The butler showing his white head at the door, his master beckoned to him.

"Tomaso, bring some Sunshine!" said he.

The readiest method of obeying this order, one might suppose, would have been, to fling wide the green window-blinds, and let the glow of the summer noon into the carefully shaded room. But, at Monte Beni, with provident caution against the wintry days, when there is little sunshine, and the rainy ones, when there is none, it was the hereditary custom to keep their Sunshine stored away in the cellar. Old Tomaso quickly produced some of it in a small, straw-covered flask, out of which he extracted the cork, and inserted a little cotton wool, to absorb the olive oil that kept the precious liquid from the air.

"This is a wine," observed the count, "the secret of making which has been kept in our family for centuries upon centuries; nor would it avail any man to steal the secret, unless he could also steal the vineyard, in which alone the Monte Beni grape can be produced. There is little else left me, save that patch of vines. Taste some of their juice, and tell me whether it is worthy to be called Sunshine! for that is its name."

"A glorious name, too!" cried the sculptor.

"Taste it," said Donatello, filling his friend's glass and pouring likewise a little into his own. "But first smell its fragrance; for the wine is very lavish of it, and will scatter it all abroad."

"Ah, how exquisite!" said Kenyon. "No other wine has a bouquet like this. The flavour must be rare indeed, if it fulfil the promise of this fragrance, which is like the airy sweetness of youthful hopes, that no realities will ever satisfy!"

This invaluable liquor was of a pale golden hue, like other of the rarest Italian wines, and, if carelessly and irreligiously quaffed, might have been mistaken for a very fine sort of Champagne. It was not, however, an effervescing wine, although its delicate piquancy produced a somewhat similar effect upon the palate. Sipping, the guest longed to sip again; but the wine demanded so deliberate a pause, in order to detect the hidden peculiarities and subtle exquisiteness of its flavour, that to drink it was really more a moral than a physical enjoyment. There was a deliciousness in it that eluded analysis, and—like whatever else is superlatively good—was perhaps better appreciated in the memory than by present consciousness. One of its most ethereal charms lay in the transitory life of the wine's richest qualities; for, while it required a certain leisure and delay, yet, if you lingered too long upon the draught, it became disenchanted both of its fragrance and its flavour.

The lustre should not be forgotten, among the other admirable endowments of the Monte Beni wine; for, as it stood in Kenyon's glass, a little circle of light glowed on the table round about it, as if it were really so much golden sunshine.

"I feel myself a better man for that ethereal potation," observed the sculptor. "The finest Orvieto, or that famous wine, the Est Est Est of Montefiascone, is vulgar in comparison. This is surely the wine of the Golden Age, such as Bacchus himself first taught mankind to press from the choicest of his grapes. My dear count, why is it not illustrious? The pale, liquid gold, in every such flask as that, might be solidified into golden scudi, and would quickly make you a millionnaire!"

Tomaso, the old butler, who was standing by the table, and enjoying the praises of the wine quite as much as if bestowed upon himself, made answer,—

"We have a tradition, signore," said he, "that this rare wine of our vineyard would lose all its wonderful qualities, if any of it were sent to market. The Counts of Monte Beni have never parted with a single flask of it for gold. At their banquets, in the olden time, they have entertained princes, cardinals, and once an emperor, and once a pope, with this delicious wine, and always, even to this day, it has been their custom to let it flow freely, when those whom they love and honour sit at the board. But the grand duke himself could not drink that wine, except it were under this very roof!"

"What you tell me, my good friend," replied Kenyon, "makes me venerate the Sunshine of Monte Beni even more abundantly than before. As I understand you, it is a sort of consecrated juice, and symbolizes the holy virtues of hospitality and social kindness?"

"Why, partly so, signore," said the old butler, with a shrewd twinkle in his eye: "but, to speak out all the truth, there is another excellent reason why neither a cask nor a flask of our precious vintage should ever be sent to market. The wine, signore, is so fond of its native home, that a transportation of even a few miles, turns it quite sour. And yet it is a wine that keeps well in the cellar, underneath this floor, and gathers fragrance, flavour, and brightness in its dark dungeon. That very flask of Sunshine, now, has kept itself for you, sir guest (as a maid reserves her sweetness till her lover comes for it), ever since a merry vintage-time, when the Signor Count here was a boy!"

"You must not wait for Tomaso to end his discourse about the wine, before drinking off your glass," observed Donatello. "When once the flask is uncorked, its finest qualities lose little time in making their escape. I doubt whether your last sip will be quite so delicious as you found the first."

And, in truth, the sculptor fancied that the Sunshine became almost imperceptibly clouded, as he approached the bottom of the flask. The effect of the wine, however, was a gentle exhilaration, which did not so speedily pass away.

Being thus refreshed, Kenyon looked around him at the antique saloon in which they sat. It was constructed in a most ponderous style, with a stone floor, on which heavy pilasters were planted against the wall, supporting arches that crossed one another in the vaulted ceiling. The upright walls, as well as the compartments of the roof, were completely covered with frescoes, which doubtless had been brilliant when first executed, and perhaps for generations afterwards. The designs were of a festive and joyous character, representing Arcadian scenes, where nymphs, fauns, and satyrs, disported themselves among mortal youths and maidens; and Pan, and the god of wine, and he of sunshine and music, disdained not to brighten some sylvan merry-making with the scarcely veiled glory of their presence. A wreath of dancing figures, in admirable variety of shape and motion, was festooned quite round the cornice of the room.

In its first splendour, the saloon must have presented

an aspect both gorgeous and enlivening; for it invested some of the cheerfullest ideas and emotions of which the human mind is susceptible with the external reality of beautiful form, and rich, harmonious glow and variety of colour. But the frescoes were now very ancient. They had been rubbed and scrubbed by old Stella and many a predecessor, and had been defaced in one spot, and retouched in another, and had peeled from the wall in patches, and had hidden some of their brightest portions under dreary dust, till the joyousness had quite vanished out of them all. It was often difficult to puzzle out the design; and even where it was more readily intelligible, the figures showed like the ghosts of dead and buried joys—the closer their resemblance to the happy past, the gloomier now. For it is thus, that with only an inconsiderable change, the gladdest objects and existences become the saddest: hope fading into disappointment; joy darkening into grief, and festal splendour into funereal duskiness: and all evolving, as their moral, a grim identity between gay things and sorrowful ones. Only give them a little time, and they turn out to be just alike!

"There has been much festivity in this saloon, if I may judge by the character of its frescoes," remarked Kenyon, whose spirits were still upheld by the mild potency of the Monte Beni wine. "Your forefathers, my dear count, must have been joyous fellows, keeping up the vintage merriment throughout the year. It does me good to think of them gladdening the hearts of men and women, with their wine of Sunshine, even in the Iron age, as Pan and Bacchus, whom we see yonder, did in the Golden one!"

"Yes: there have been merry times in the banquet-hall of Monte Beni, even within my own remembrance," replied Donatello, looking gravely at the painted walls. "It was meant for mirth, as you see: and when I brought my own cheerfulness into the saloon, these frescoes looked cheerful too. But methinks they have all faded since I saw them last."

"It would be a good idea," said the sculptor, falling into his companion's vein, and helping him out with an illustration which Donatello himself could not have put into shape, "to convert this saloon into a chapel; and when the priest tells his hearers of the instability of earthly joys, and would show how drearily they vanish, he may point to these pictures, that were so joyous, and are so dismal. He could not illustrate his theme so aptly in any other way."

"True, indeed," answered the count, his former simplicity strangely mixing itself up with an experience that had changed him; "and yonder, where the minstrels used to stand, the altar shall be placed. A sinful man might do all the more effective penance in this old banquet-hall."

"But I should regret to have suggested so ungenial a transformation in your hospitable saloon," continued Kenyon, duly noting the change in Donatello's characteristics. "You startle me, my friend, by so ascetic a design! It would hardly have entered your head, when we first met. Pray do not—if I may take the freedom of a somewhat elder man to advise you," added he, smiling—"pray do not, under a notion of improvement, take upon yourself to be sombre, thoughtful, and penitential, like all the rest of us."

Donatello made no answer, but sat awhile, appearing to follow with his eyes one of the figures, which was repeated many times over in the groups upon the walls and ceiling. It formed the principal link of an allegory, by which (as is often the case in such pictorial designs) the whole series of frescoes were bound together, but which it would be impossible, or, at least, very wearisome, to unravel. The sculptor's eyes took a similar direction, and soon began to trace through the vicissitudes—once gay, now sombre—in which the old artist had involved it, the same individual figure. He fancied a resemblance in it to Donatello himself; and it put him in mind of one of the purposes with which he had come to Monte Beni.

"My dear count," said he, "I have a proposal to make. You must let me employ a little of my leisure in modelling your bust. You remember what a striking resemblance we all of us—Hilda, Miriam, and I—found between your features and those of the Faun of Praxiteles. Then, it seemed an identity; but now that I know your face better, the likeness is far less apparent. Your head in marble would be a treasure to me. Shall I have it?"

"I have a weakness which I fear I cannot overcome," replied the count, turning away his face. "It troubles me to be looked at steadfastly."

"I have observed it since we have been sitting here, though never before," rejoined the sculptor. "It is a kind of nervousness, I apprehend, which you caught in the Roman air, and which grows upon you, in your solitary life. It need be no hindrance to my taking your bust; for I will catch the likeness and expression by side glimpses, which (if portrait painters and bust makers did but know it) always bring home richer results than a broad stare."

"You may take me if you have the power," said Donatello; but, even as he spoke, he turned away his face; "and if you can see what makes me shrink from you, you are welcome to put it in the bust. It is not my will, but my necessity, to avoid men's eyes. Only," he added, with a smile which made Kenyon doubt whether he might not as well copy the Faun as model a new bust, "only, you know, you must not insist on my uncovering these ears of mine!"

"Nay; I never should dream of such a thing," answered the sculptor, laughing as the young count shook his clustering curls. "I could not hope to persuade you, remembering how Miriam once failed!"

Nothing is more unaccountable than the spell that often lurks in a spoken word. A thought may be present to the mind, so distinctly that no utterance could make it more so; and two minds may be conscious of the same thought, in which one or both take the profoundest interest; but as long as it remains unspoken, their familiar talk flows quietly over the hidden idea, as a rivulet may sparkle and dimple over something sunken in its bed. But, speak the word; and it is like bringing up a drowned body out of the deepest pool of the rivulet, which has been aware of the horrible secret all along, in spite of its smiling surface.

And even so, when Kenyon chanced to make a distinct reference to Donatello's relations with Miriam (though the subject was already in both their minds), a ghastly emotion rose up out of the depths of the young count's heart. He trembled either with anger or terror, and glared at the sculptor with wild eyes, like a wolf that meets you in the forest, and hesitates whether to flee or turn to bay. But, as Kenyon still looked calmly at him, his aspect gradually became less disturbed, though far from resuming its former quietude.

"You have spoken her name," said he, at last, in an altered and tremulous tone; "tell me, now, all that you know of her."

"I scarcely think that I have any later intelligence than yourself," answered Kenyon; "Miriam left Rome at about the time of your own departure. Within a day or two after our last meeting at the church of the Capuchins, I called at her studio and found it vacant. Whither she has gone, I cannot tell."

Donatello asked no further questions.

They rose from table, and strolled together about the premises, whiling away the afternoon with brief intervals of unsatisfactory conversation, and many shadowy silences. The sculptor had a perception of change in his companion—possibly of growth and development, but certainly of change—which saddened him, because it took away much of the simple grace that was the best of Donatello's peculiarities.

Kenyon betook himself to repose that night in a grim, old, vaulted apartment, which, in the lapse of five or six centuries, had probably been the birth, bridal, and death chamber of a great many generations of the Monte Beni family. He was aroused, soon after daylight, by the clamour of a tribe of beggars who had taken their stand in a little rustic lane that crept beside that portion of the villa, and were addressing their petitions to the open windows. By and by, they appeared to have received alms, and took their departure.

"Some charitable Christian has sent those vagabonds away," thought the sculptor, as he resumed his interrupted nap: "who could it be? Donatello has his own rooms in the tower; Stella, Tomaso, and the cook are a world's width off; and I fancied myself the only inhabitant in this part of the house."

In the breadth and space which so delightfully characterize an Italian villa, a dozen guests might have had each his suite of apartments without infringing upon one another's ample precincts. But, so far as Kenyon knew, he was the only visitor beneath Donatello's widely extended roof.

CHAPTER XXVI.

The Pedigree of Monte Beni.

FROM the old butler, whom he found to be a very gracious and affable personage, Kenyon soon learned many curious particulars about the family history and hereditary peculiarities of the Counts of Monte Beni. There was a pedigree, the later portion of which—that is to say, for a little more than a thousand years—a genealogist would have found delight in tracing out, link by link, and authenticating by records and documentary evidences. It would have been as difficult, however, to follow up the stream of Donatello's ancestry to its dim source, as travellers have found it to reach the mysterious fountains of the Nile. And, far beyond the region of definite and demonstrable fact, a romancer might have strayed into a region of old poetry, where the rich soil, so long uncultivated and untrodden, had lapsed into nearly its primeval state of wilderness. Among those antique paths, now overgrown with tangled and riotous vegetation, the wanderer must needs follow his own guidance, and arrive nowhither at last.

The race of Monte Beni, beyond a doubt, was one of the oldest in Italy, where families appear to survive at least, if not to flourish, on their half-decayed roots, oftener than in England or France. It came down in a broad track from the Middle Ages; but, at epochs anterior to those, it was distinctly visible in the gloom of the period before chivalry put forth its flower; and farther still, we are almost afraid to say, it was seen, though with a fainter and wavering course, in the early morn of Christendom, when the Roman Empire had hardly begun to show symptoms of decline. At that venerable distance, the heralds gave up the lineage in despair.

But where written record left the genealogy of Monte Beni, tradition took it up, and carried it without dread or shame beyond the Imperial ages into the times of the Roman republic; beyond those, again, into the epoch of kingly rule. Nor even so remotely among the mossy centuries did it pause, but strayed onward into that gray antiquity of which there is no token left, save its cavernous tombs, and a few bronzes, and some quaintly wrought ornaments of gold, and gems with mystic figures and inscriptions. There, or thereabouts, the line was supposed to have had its origin in the sylvan life of Etruria, while Italy was yet guiltless of Rome.

Of course, as we regret to say, the earlier and very much the larger portion of this respectable descent—and the same is true of many briefer pedigrees—must be looked upon as altogether mythical. Still, it threw a romantic interest around the unquestionable antiquity of the Monte Beni family, and over that tract of their own vines and fig-trees, beneath the shade of which they had unquestionably dwelt for immemorial ages. And there they had laid the foundations of their tower, so long ago that one-half of its height was said to be sunken under the surface and to hide subterranean chambers which once were cheerful with the olden sunshine.

One story, or myth, that had mixed itself up with their mouldy genealogy, interested the sculptor by its wild, and perhaps grotesque, yet not unfascinating peculiarity. He caught at it the more eagerly, as it afforded a shadowy and whimsical semblance of explanation for the likeness which he, with Miriam and Hilda, had seen, or fancied, between Donatello and the Faun of Praxiteles.

The Monte Beni family, as this legend averred, drew their origin from the Pelasgic race, who peopled Italy in times that may be called pre-historic. It was the same noble breed of men, of Asiatic birth, that settled in Greece; the same happy and poetic kindred who dwelt in Arcadia, and — whether they ever lived such life or not—enriched the world with dreams, at least, and fables, lovely, if unsubstantial, of a Golden Age. In those delicious times, when deities and demigods appeared familiarly on earth, mingling with its inhabitants as friend with friend—when nymphs, satyrs, and the whole train of classic faith or fable, hardly took pains to hide themselves in the primeval woods—at that auspicious period the lineage of Monte Beni had its rise. Its progenitor was a being not altogether human, yet partaking so largely of the gentlest human qualities, as to be neither awful nor shocking to the imagination. A sylvan creature, native among the woods, had loved a mortal maiden, and—perhaps by kindness, and the subtle courtesies which love might teach to his simplicity, or possibly by a ruder wooing—had won her to his haunts. In due time, he gained her womanly affection; and, making their bridal bower, for aught we know, in the hollow of a great tree, the pair spent a happy wedded life in that ancient neighbourhood where now stood Donatello's tower.

From this union sprang a vigorous progeny that took its place unquestioned among human families. In that age, however, and long afterwards, it showed the ineffaceable lineaments of its wild paternity: it was a pleasant and kindly race of men, but capable of savage fierceness, and never quite restrainable within the trammels of social law. They were strong, active, genial, cheerful as the sunshine, passionate as the tornado. Their lives were rendered blissful by an unsought harmony with nature.

But, as centuries passed away, the Faun's wild blood had necessarily been attempered with constant intermixtures from the more ordinary streams of human life. It lost many of its original qualities, and served, for the most part, only to bestow an unconquerable vigour which kept the family from extinction, and enabled them to make their own part good throughout the perils and rude emergencies of their interminable descent. In the constant wars with which Italy was plagued, by the dissensions of her petty states and republics, there was a demand for native hardihood.

The successive members of the Monte Beni family showed valour and policy enough, at all events, to keep their hereditary possessions out of the clutch of grasping neighbours, and probably differed very little from the other feudal barons with whom they fought and feasted. Such a degree of conformity with the manners of the generations, through which it survived, must have been essential to the prolonged continuance of the race.

It is well known, however that any hereditary peculiarity—as a supernumerary finger, or an anomalous shape of feature, like the Austrian lip—is wont to show itself in a family after a very wayward fashion. It skips at its own pleasure along the line, and, latent for half a century or so, crops out again in a great-grandson. And thus, it was said, from a period beyond memory or record, there had ever and anon been a descendant of the Monte Benis bearing nearly all the characteristics that were attributed to the original founder of the race. Some traditions even went so far as to enumerate the ears, covered with a delicate fur, and shaped like a pointed leaf, among the proofs of authentic descent which were seen in these favoured individuals. We appreciate the beauty of such tokens of a nearer kindred to the great family of nature than other mortals bear; but it would be idle to ask credit for a statement which might be deemed to partake so largely of the grotesque.

But it was indisputable that, once in a century, or oftener, a son of Monte Beni gathered into himself the scattered qualities of his race, and reproduced the character that had been assigned to it from immemorial times. Beautiful, strong, brave, kindly, sincere, of honest impulses, and endowed with simple tastes and the love of homely pleasures, he was believed to possess gifts by which he could associate himself with the wild things of the forests, and with the fowls of the air, and could feel a sympathy even with the trees, among which it was his joy to dwell. On the other hand, there were deficiencies both of intellect and heart, and especially, as it seemed, in the development of the higher portion of man's nature. These defects were less perceptible in early youth, but showed themselves more strongly with advancing age, when, as the animal spirits settled down upon a lower level, the representative of the Monte Benis was apt to become sensual, addicted to gross pleasures, heavy, unsympathizing, and insulated within the narrow limits of a surly selfishness.

A similar change, indeed, is no more than what we constantly observe to take place in persons who are not careful to substitute other graces for those which they inevitably lose along with the quick sensibility and joyous vivacity of youth. At worst, the reigning Count of Monte Beni, as his hair grew white, was still a jolly old fellow over his flask of wine—the wine that Bacchus himself was fabled to have taught his sylvan ancestor how to express, and from what choicest grapes, which would ripen only in a certain divinely favoured portion of the Monte Beni vineyard.

The family, be it observed, were both proud and ashamed of these legends; but whatever part of them they might consent to incorporate into their ancestral history, they steadily repudiated all that referred to their one distinctive feature, the pointed and furry ears. In a great many years past, no sober credence had been yielded to the mythical portion of the pedigree. It might, however, be considered as typifying some such assemblage of qualities—in this case, chiefly remarkable for their simplicity and naturalness—as, when they reappear in successive generations, constitute what we call family character. The sculptor found, moreover, on the evidence of some old portraits, that the physical features of the race had long been similar to what he now saw them in Donatello. With accumulating years, it is true, the Monte Beni face had a tendency to look grim and savage; and, in two or three instances, the family pictures glared at the spectator in the eyes like some surly animal, that had lost its good-humour when it outlived its playfulness.

The young count accorded his guest full liberty to investigate the personal annals of these pictured worthies, as well as all the rest of his progenitors; and ample materials were at hand in many chests of worm-eaten papers and yellow parchments, that had been gathering into larger and dustier piles ever since the dark ages. But, to confess the truth, the information afforded by these musty documents was so much more prosaic than what Kenyon acquired from Tomaso's legends, that even the superior authenticity of the former could not reconcile him to its dulness.

What especially delighted the sculptor, was the

analogy between Donatello's character, as he himself knew it, and those peculiar traits which the old butler's narrative assumed to have been long hereditary in the race. He was amused at finding, too, that not only Tomaso but the peasantry of the estate and neighbouring village recognized his friend as a genuine Monte Beni, of the original type. They seemed to cherish a great affection for the young count, and were full of stories about his sportive childhood; how he had played among the little rustics, and been at once the wildest and the sweetest of them all; and how, in his very infancy, he had plunged into the deep pools of the streamlets and never been drowned, and had clambered to the topmost branches of tall trees without ever breaking his neck. No such mischance could happen to the sylvan child, because, handling all the elements of nature so fearlessly and freely, nothing had either the power or the will to do him harm.

He grew up, said these humble friends, the playmate not only of all mortal kind, but of creatures of the woods; although, when Kenyon pressed them for some particulars of this latter mode of companionship, they could remember little more than a few anecdotes of a pet fox, which used to growl and snap at everybody save Donatello himself.

But they enlarged—and never were weary of the theme—upon the blithesome effects of Donatello's presence in his rosy childhood and budding youth. Their hovels had always glowed like sunshine when he entered them; so that, as the peasants expressed it, their young master had never darkened a doorway in his life. He was the soul of vintage festivals. While he was a mere infant, scarcely able to run alone, it had been the custom to make him tread the wine-press with his tender little feet, if it were only to crush one cluster of the grapes. And the grape-juice that gushed beneath his childish tread, be it ever so small in quantity, sufficed to impart a pleasant flavour to a whole cask of wine. The race of Monte Beni—so these rustic chroniclers assured the sculptor—had possessed the gift from the oldest of old times of expressing good wine from ordinary grapes, and a ravishing liquor from the choice growth of their vineyard.

In a word, as he listened to such tales as these, Kenyon could have imagined that the valleys and hill-sides about him were a veritable Arcadia, and that Donatello was not merely a sylvan faun, but the genial wine-god in his very person. Making many allowances for the poetic fancies of Italian peasants, he set it down for fact, that his friend, in a simple way, and among rustic folks, had been an exceedingly delightful fellow in his younger days.

But the contadini sometimes added, shaking their heads and sighing, that the young count was sadly changed since he went to Rome. The village girls now missed the merry smile with which he used to greet them.

The sculptor inquired of his good friend Tomaso, whether he, too, had noticed the shadow which was said to have recently fallen over Donatello's life.

"Ah, yes, signor!" answered the old butler, "it is even so, since he came back from that wicked and miserable city. The world has grown either too evil, or else too wise and sad, for such men as the old Counts of Monte Beni used to be. His very first taste of it, as you see, has changed and spoilt my poor young lord. There had not been a single count in the family these hundred years and more, who was so true a Monte Beni, of the antique stamp, as this poor signorino; and now it brings the tears into my eyes to hear him sighing over a cup of Sunshine! Ah, it is a sad world now!"

"Then you think there was a merrier world once?" asked Kenyon.

"Surely, signor," said Tomaso; "a merrier world, and merrier Counts of Monte Beni to live in it! Such tales of them as I have heard, when I was a child on my grandfather's knee! The good old man remembered a lord of Monte Beni—at least, he had heard of such a one, though I will not make oath upon the holy crucifix that my grandsire lived in his time—who used to go into the woods and call pretty damsels out of the fountains, and out of the trunks of the old trees. That merry lord was known to dance with them a whole long summer afternoon! When shall we see such frolics in our days?"

"Not soon, I am afraid," acquiesced the sculptor. "You are right, excellent Tomaso: the world is sadder now!"

And, in truth, while our friend smiled at these wild

ſables, he sighed in the same breath to think how the once genial earth produces, in every successive generation, ſewer flowers than used to gladden the preceding ones. Not that the modes and seeming possibilities of human enjoyment are rarer in our refined and softened era—on the contrary, they never beſore were nearly so abundant—but that mankind are getting so ſar beyond the childhood of their race that they scorn to be happy any longer. A simple and joyous character can find no place for itselſ among the sage and sombre figures that would put his unsophisticated cheerfulness to shame. The entire system oſ man's aſſairs, as at present established, is built up purposely to exclude the careless and happy soul. The very children would upbraid the wretched individual who should endeavour to take life and the world as—what we might naturally suppose them meant ſor—a place and opportunity ſor enjoyment.

It is the iron rule in our day to require an object and a purpose in liſe. It makes us all parts oſ a complicated scheme oſ progress, which can only result in our arrival at a colder and drearier region than we were born in. It insists upon everybody's adding somewhat—a mite, perhaps, but earned by incessant eſſort—to an accumulated pile oſ usefulness, oſ which the only use will be, to burden our posterity with even heavier thoughts and more inordinate labour than our own. No liſe now wanders like an unſettered stream; there is a mill-wheel ſor the tiniest rivulet to turn. We go all wrong, by too strenuous a resolution to go all right,

Therefore it was—so, at least, the sculptor thought, although partly suspicious of Donatello's darker misfortune—that the young count found it impossible now-a-days to be what his forefathers had been. He could not live their healthy life of animal spirits, in their sympathy with nature, and brotherhood with all that breathed around them. Nature, in beast, fowl, and tree, and earth, flood, and sky, is what it was of old; but sin, care, and self-consciousness have set the human portion of the world askew; and thus the simplest character is ever the soonest to go astray.

"At any rate, Tomaso," said Kenyon, doing his best to comfort the old man, "let us hope that your young lord will still enjoy himself at vintage-time. By the aspect of the vineyard, I judge that this will be a famous year for the golden wine of Monte Beni. As long as your grapes produce that admirable liquor, sad as you think the world, neither the count nor his guests will quite forget to smile."

"Ah, signor," rejoined the butler with a sigh, "but he scarcely wets his lips with the sunny juice."

"There is yet another hope," observed Kenyon; "the young count may fall in love, and bring home a fair and laughing wife to chase the gloom out of yonder old, frescoed saloon. Do you think he could do a better thing, my good Tomaso?"

"Maybe not, signor," said the sage butler, looking earnestly at him; "and, maybe, not a worse!"

The sculptor fancied that the good old man had it partly in his mind to make some remark, or communicate some fact, which, on second thoughts, he resolved to keep concealed in his own breast. He now took his departure cellarward, shaking his white head and muttering to himself, and did not reappear till dinner-time, when he favoured Kenyon, whom he had taken far into his good graces, with a choicer flask of Sunshine than had yet blessed his palate.

To say the truth, this golden wine was no unnecessary ingredient towards making the life of Monte Beni palatable. It seemed a pity that Donatello did not drink a little more of it, and go jollily to bed at least, even if he should awake with an accession of darker melancholy the next morning.

Nevertheless, there was no lack of outward means for leading an agreeable life in the old villa. Wandering musicians haunted the precincts of Monte Beni, where they seemed to claim a prescriptive right; they made the lawn and shrubbery tuneful with the sound of fiddle, harp, and flute, and now and then with the tangled squeaking of a bagpipe. Improvvisatori likewise came and told tales or recited verses to the contadini—among whom Kenyon often was an auditor—after their day's work in the vineyard. Jugglers, too, obtained permission to do feats of magic in the hall, where they set even the sage Tomaso, and Stella, Girolamo, and the peasant girls from the farmhouse, all of a broad grin, between merriment and wonder. These good people got food and lodging for their pleasant pains, and some of the small wine of Tuscany, and a reasonable handful of the Grand Duke's copper coin, to keep up the hospitable renown of Monte Beni. But very seldom had they the young count as a listener, or a spectator.

There were sometimes dances by moonlight on the lawn, but never since he came from Rome did Donatello's presence deepen the blushes of the pretty contadinas, or his footstep weary out the most agile partner or competitor, as once it was sure to do.

Paupers—for this kind of vermin infested the house of Monte Beni worse than any other spot in beggar-haunted Italy—stood beneath all the windows, making loud supplication, or even establishing themselves on the marble steps of the grand entrance. They ate and drank, and filled their bags, and pocketed the little money that was given them, and went forth on their devious ways, showering blessings innumerable on the mansion and its lord, and on the souls of his deceased forefathers, who had always been just such simpletons as to be compassionate to beggary. But, in spite of their favourable prayers—by which Italian philanthropists set great store—a cloud seemed to hang over these once Arcadian precincts, and to be darkest around the summit of the tower where Donatello was wont to sit and brood.

END OF VOL. I.

PRINTING OFFICE OF THE PUBLISHER.

www.ingramcontent.com/pod-product-compliance
Lightning Source LLC
Chambersburg PA
CBHW021212270326
41929CB00010B/1088
9783741162985